The Human's
Handbook

An Owner's Manual for People

MARIAN ROSE GLASS

BALBOA.
PRESS

A DIVISION OF HAY HOUSE

Balboa Press books may be ordered through booksellers or by contacting:

Balboa Press
A Division of Hay House
1663 Liberty Drive
Bloomington, IN 47403
www.balboapress.com
1 (877) 407-4847

Because of the dynamic nature of the Internet, any web addresses or
links contained in this book may have changed since publication and
may no longer be valid. The views expressed in this work are solely those
of the author and do not necessarily reflect the views of the publisher,
and the publisher hereby disclaims any responsibility for them.

The author of this book does not dispense medical advice or prescribe the use
of any technique as a form of treatment for physical, emotional, or medical
problems without the advice of a physician, either directly or indirectly. The
intent of the author is only to offer information of a general nature to help
you in your quest for emotional and spiritual well-being. In the event you use
any of the information in this book for yourself, which is your constitutional
right, the author and the publisher assume no responsibility for your actions.

Any people depicted in stock imagery provided by Thinkstock are
models, and such images are being used for illustrative purposes only.
Certain stock imagery © Thinkstock.

Printed in the United States of America.

ISBN: 978-1-4525-2346-0 (sc)
ISBN: 978-1-4525-2347-7 (e)

Balboa Press rev. date: 10/22/2014

At 81 years of age, Marian Glass enjoys
ballroom dancing to stay young and strong.

ACKNOWLEDGEMENTS

First, a great thank you to my dear friend, Louise Giuliano, for all the time and effort she put in to printing and reprinting the manuscript and editing my errors.

Next, my gratitude to all the humans who contributed, some knowingly and others unknowingly, to the information contained in this work.

Mostly, to Divine Mind which filled *my* mind with the wisdom and understanding to write down the enlightenment given me page after page. It is meant to be shared. **Use it well.**

It is now the year 2014 and publishing time. Five more people have entered the scene: My friend Joe Nash over at the Sanford Library, who always has the encouraging words. My three computer angels: Bethany Koehn, Rita Russell, and Holly Livingston.

And last but most—Steve Ribner, my friend the enabler, without whose amazing patience and skill this work could not have come to fruition, I am so grateful!

M. Glass

TABLE (?) OF CONTENTS

Oh well, read the whole book.

It's all relevant....
from fetus to elderly.

It could change your life for the better and maybe
the world we live in as well.

We have to try.

M. Glass

AN IDEA GREW

Introduction

The idea for this book was born a few years ago when I came to live in a "senior citizens" apartment house. I had rented the apartment from 2400 miles away while living in Tucson, Arizona. My hometown of Albany, New York seemed to beckon me after 37 years of living in various other places. Since I was 68 years old at the time of my return to my roots, I felt that a senior building would be appropriate for me. I had been told that it was a lovely 12 story high-rise in a beautiful neighborhood and had all sorts of amenities (not an assisted living building, but one with security and convenient living). I was and still am a very active person, was still working at a junior college in Tucson, driving my own car and attending dances, theatre, lectures, family outings, giving a class at the Udall Center on fitness, and in perfect health.

Upon my arrival in Albany in April 1995, I had my introduction in person to my new abode. A parade of walkers, people with canes, people bent over with osteoporosis, people in wheelchairs and those who seemed to be managing on their own in somewhat perpendicular positions...greeted my astonished eyes.

I pause now living over the disappointment I felt... OK.

Being a resilient and resourceful person, I set about making my efficiency apartment not only efficient, but also quite lovely and my sanctuary apart from all the sickness and degeneration around me. Some of these other residents were not much older than I (in fact hardly at all), but for some reasons they had aged and become seriously ill. I had to find out why.

I made friends with some of the more pleasant residents, and although most of them were hard of hearing and I had to repeat and shout to carry on a conversation, I kept persevering––but it was not easy. Finally, I got the idea to return to one of my previous careers of giving motivational talks and volunteered to give a series of lectures for seven weeks in the community room at the apartment house. I had standing room only for the first lecture (they came out of curiosity) and then the apathy set in and only about a couple dozen of the more open-minded kept attending. Actually that was some kind of miracle, I realized later, when lecturers from the various medical centers were invited to speak here, and only 13 residents showed out of 220.

The following autumn, I was asked to hold discussion groups weekly in the small community room and about a dozen of the more amiable residents became loyal participants. We discussed only "up" things like what interests would they like to pursue, and it led to our publishing a sort of bimonthly newspaper about eight pages long with poetry and inspiring articles, which we distributed throughout the building (211 apartments). It was very well received, and we were all gratified. Only women got involved with the project for some odd (?) reason.

At one of the meetings of the discussion group, I let it be known that for some time I had been toying with the idea of writing an Owner's Manual for People and would entitle it THE HUMAN'S HANDBOOK. The group members got very interested in the idea and wanted to contribute some thoughts of their own. I made notes and the EASY OUTLINE came from that outpouring of thoughts.

The longer I lived there and the more people I became friendly with convinced me that human beings need to get in control of their minds and their lives and take responsibility for their well-being and lifestyle.

AND furthermore, I will not be allowed to make my next transition until I complete this. Not to sound morbid, for I know transition is not sadness but a joy, I keep asking God if I did enough yet to graduate. I feel so ready to move on to a better plateau. Did I do enough??? OK now get this published and distributed around the globe... in whatever language works for each area.

Marian R. Glass
8/11/98

CONTENTS

AN OWNER'S MANUAL FOR PEOPLE

By Marian R. Glass

Well, why not? We have owner's manuals for cars, stereos, VCRs and even my little kitchen toaster. BUT for the most important thing we own (ourselves), we do not have a manual.

Without an owner's manual for US we really cannot expect to know how to "operate" this thing we call our body and especially our mind. So we start right off making all kinds of errors in the care and maintenance of US by eating unhealthful foods and drinking harmful liquids; and not being aware of breathing in "bad air" (like tobacco smoke and car exhaust) and not exercising properly or often enough (or improperly and too much) and perhaps most importantly of all playing host to erroneous thoughts... just for starts.

O.K... I realize that as a baby you had to ingest whatever was supplied and had no choice and probably no complaints that would make any difference. However, as soon as possible when you are so enabled to make choices, you need to know what to reject and what to insist on having. Hopefully this book will help future generations to make better choices. Some of the information is for the parents, obviously, but then very early in life a child should be made aware of the dangers of not taking good care of the body and mind. Learn for yourself and your children and then allow children access to this guidance directly...when reading comprehension is achieved.

We have only to examine ourselves and observe others to realize the devastating effect of abusing our body and mind. We cannot expect our body and our mind to serve us well if we do not care for them well. We pay the price for our errors in all sorts of illnesses and incapacities. Surely we do not want this to continue. We do not want to do any more damage to ourselves and certainly want to prevent any damage to the children. Most of the information herein is so practical, so logical, and so sensible, that one wonders why its practical application is so widely ignored.

It must be time to let the light in or I wouldn't be sitting here typing this manuscript...on the whole I would rather be out dancing. At 70 years young, I still dance like a 20 year old (so I'm told) and pass for about 50. I tell you folks we can repair and good living is the answer. I am going to share with you in all the pages to follow the wondrous and seemingly miraculous happenings that can be part of your life too. Living healthfully is actually fun!

FIRST THING FIRST

Before we can operate our body properly, we must know how to operate our mind. Everything begins in mind (thought) and please keep that in mind before you make manifest physically any damaging thoughts. In other words "Thoughts kept in mind, reproduce in kind". Negative thinking produces negative results, and so it must follow that the good, the positive, the beautiful thoughts produce their beneficial results. Try it; you will like it.

Most of the harmful thoughts we harbor have been passed down to us through the generations...old wives' tales, myths, archaic beliefs, and the like. These must be destroyed before they destroy us. In other words, we must wipe the slate clean to receive new information, or in more modern terms, erase the memory in our mental computer to receive improved data. And again, this is an invigorating process that brings about a wondrous feeling of release and relief. Not to carry around the limiting and harmful burden of false information is like being set free to lead a healthier more fulfilling life...and that is exactly what happens.

Later in this book there is a complete chapter on "Myths and Misinformation" from "Aging" to our complete belief system, but for now it seems important to point out some high (or low) points that need attention immediately.

Marian Rose Glass

Do you know that the human race has accepted a far more rapid aging process than was intended? As young as 40, there are men and women who must resort to plastic surgery to have the appearance of youth (At 40, I looked 25). What is their problem? Well, I'll tell you. They looked at pictures of their parents, or even their grandparents, as they were aging (in their misinformed minds) and mentally copied the picture, until at last it reproduced itself in them. THOUGHT IS MORE POWERFUL THAN YOU KNOW! How about looking at pictures of yourself at a younger age and keeping that in mind. Use that as your guide to the appearance you desire. The ancient Greeks kept beautiful statues and paintings around them so that vision was in their mind to be emulated. Smart!

Although everything does begin in thought, we must follow through with appropriate behavior. We cannot stuff ourselves with junk food (or even with too much good food). We cannot imbibe potent potables (get drunk). We cannot use tobacco in any form; we cannot drug our minds. We cannot sop up caffeine; to name a few of the poisons and bad habits...and expect to look good, feel well and have good vitality and...think clearly! All of that is learned behavior and would not come naturally to you if not passed down to you. Think about that! Please! None of these destructive habits were inborn. You developed them through misguidance and pressures of an ignorant society. Let it stop here...and now! We cannot afford to cause any more damage to the human race.

We speak of built-in obsolescence regarding the machines we own, and as true as it appears to be in manufactured goods, this description could be applied to us humans. None of us is going to last forever, but it is the quality of life while it is within us that brings fulfillment and happiness. A mind muddled by drugs and alcohol cannot produce the highest quality of life. A body carrying excess weight, or having eating disorders, will not serve us very well for long. Misuse or non-use of the body will cause deterioration. If not exercised properly you could be very old before your time. So think youth and vitality and follow through with living it. It is part of the wisdom of life.

Unlike the machines that come from the factory already manufactured, or just ready to be assembled, we humans are manufacturing ourselves. We are not only building a body but a mind (and a soul, which we will examine later in the book). The body is like soft clay that we are able to mold if we know that we have this ability. What masterpiece are you creating? Where are your thoughts taking you? Your thoughts precede action. You can see why it is so necessary to put the mind in good working order so that it produces the you that you truly want to be. "Visualize and actualize" is a really workable process. If you cannot visualize clearly, take pictures from magazines showing what it is that you would like to actualize (make happen) and put them in places where you can be reminded of your goals.

These things I write about are things that I use and do. Works for me! Actually, it works for thousands if not millions of people.

When I was about three years old, I caught the measles, which left me with a crossed eye. I didn't realize I looked different from other children until I entered kindergarten at age five and then got the rude awakening. All the other children had normal eyes! So I decided at that tender age that I would straighten my eye by exercising it. The eye doctor told my mother that by age nine I would be old enough for him to operate on my eye. My, was he surprised to see it had straightened out all by itself! I did not tell anyone (I don't think I would have known how to anyway), but I knew God and I had worked together to take care of my eye. Get the picture! I did. I visualized my eye corrected, so it was!

Oh! I will not wait until the end of the book to make the disclosure that I believe in God. Who do you think is dictating this anyway? That's all right...just keep reading.

One of the major obstacles to being all that we were meant to be is the idea of heredity. The idea that we have to inherit illnesses and afflictions from our family tree is horrifying and not true. We are separate and unique individuals and do not have to imitate our forefathers (and mothers) in their weakness of genes, bodily structure, mental capacity, or habits. The words "pre-disposed to" should be taken out of the vocabulary. These ideas are erroneous and have been perpetuated in ignorance.

In Dr. Sherwin Nuland's book THE WISDOM OF THE BODY he refers to spontaneous mutation, explaining that the genes do not always take the course expected. He speaks of gene expression...that we can select activators and repressors through our hormones. I picture our bodies as buffet tables from which we could choose the genes we want and ignore those we do not. In other words, we could picture our hormones selecting only the genes we feel are desirable. Both of my parents had genes that I did not wish to carry on such as mother's enlarged heart valve, arthritis, sinusitis (both parents), dad's flat feet, hardening arteries, both parents' poor dental health, and in deciding none of that was for me...my hormones must have chosen or activated better genes. I am grateful to Dr. Nuland for the scientific explanation of what I felt was my privilege as a human being. It is also yours.

In Dr. Deepak Chopra's book AGELESS BODY, TIMELESS MIND, he states, "To challenge aging at its core, this entire worldview must be challenged first, for nothing holds more power over the body than beliefs of the mind." Just one of the enlightened statements in this book opens the door of the mind and says, "come in and tell me all ...for I want to learn it all." We have such great teachers on the planet at this time. Let us not waste their wisdom.

In Dr. Abraham Maslow's book THE FARTHER REACHES OF HUMAN NATURE, he states, "Most psychiatrists and many psychologists and biologists now have come simply to assume that practically all diseases, and perhaps even all diseases without exception, can be called psychosomatic or organismic. That is, if one pursues any "physical' illness far enough and deep enough, one will find inevitably intrapsychic, interpersonal, and social variables that are also involved as determinants". In other words, folks, we do it to ourselves.

In Dr. Herbert Benson's book TIMELESS HEALING, he observes that people who have faith recover from illnesses better than those who do not. At the end of the book he has a "Disclosure" stating he believes in God. I see no harm in telling the world that I believe in God...right up front. But then I am not of the scientific world and can afford to be very spiritual openly.

Dr. Andrew Weil has contributed so much toward informing the public about the care and feeding of the human race in his books, SPONTANEOUS HEALING and EIGHT WEEKS TO OPTIMUM HEALTH.

Most of these esteemed doctors have been on television in addition to the advanced thinkers who have been interviewed by Dr. Jeffrey Mishlove on his television program THINKING ALLOWED (also a book).

There is no way I could list all the gifted thinkers and their accomplishments, but I am sincerely grateful for the effort each has put forth in trying to enlighten the human race.

So you may wonder how it could be that Marian R. Glass could sit down at a typewriter and try to add to all of the works of the masters. Well, I'll tell you. For the past 65 years (or longer) I not only have been trying to get these messages out but also I have been demonstrating the truth of the messages in my life. When during the past decade or two I discovered that there were "other minds swimming in the same Crystal River" with me (a thought from Richard Bach, whose writings I dearly love), I was absolutely ecstatic! When my friends would call and tell me about Dr. Chopra's books and his lectures on TV, my response was…"Thank God! I need all the help I can get." And my friends, knowing what my writings and lectures were about and the miracles that occurred in my life, knew exactly what I meant.

I firmly believe that there cannot be enough books, articles, lectures and TV programs expressing the enlightened ideas and truths that Divine Mind wants the human race to know.

Each of us has a different style and method of expression and if one does not get through, perhaps another will. Just a different way with words may push the right buttons that will open heretofore-closed minds. Remember a closed mind is a grave housing dead thoughts. LET NEW LIFE INTO YOUR MIND.

As long as the human race is still abusing, mis-using, dis-using and non-using the human body and mind, it would appear repetition and constant reaffirming is necessary. What a pity all this suffering and limitation is for lack of knowledge.

One truth that we all seem to agree with is that stress and/or depression when allowed to stay around too long, weakens and even shuts down the immune system leaving the human wide open to illness. I want to deal with that matter in this book, because I have been so successful myself in transcending depression when confronted by serious illness and crippling disease; emotional crises; financial difficulties and other situations that were brought on by my erroneous thoughts and beliefs. Experience is the greatest teacher, but I would like you to learn by my experience so that you do not have to suffer.

I know I am not being gender biased when I suggest that everyone, male and female, read Dr. Christiane Northrup's book WOMEN'S BODIES, WOMEN'S WISDOM. Here are some quotes from the book to give you some idea -------:

Page 58 - *"INTUITION is the direct perception of truth or fact independent of any reasoning process,"*

Page 59 - *"Our bodies are designed to function best when we are doing work that feels exactly right to us. If we want to know God's will for us, all we have to do is look to our gifts and talents – that's where we will find it."*

Page 592 - *'Without slipping into self-blame, think back on the last time you had to miss work because of illness. Was the illness a satisfying break from your routine...Do you see any way that you could get the same rest without being sick?"*

Page 657 - *"We must learn to see ourselves as processes – changing and growing over time"*

This is an excerpt from my book published in 1981, WHICH END IS UP? - Page 34. *"No little book on "How to" will be enough help. Learn to recognize the people who seem always to be depressed, angry, vengeful, untruthful, lazy and irresponsible so that you can steer clear of them. Put them out of your experience as quickly as possible...they need professional help.*

"We will come across all types of people in our adventure of this life and along the way we can demonstrate and explain

the principles that can work for most. We can set a good example by renewing our lives by renewing our mind. It is possible for this attitude to "rub off" on others. I have witnessed this happening. We are all in an endless evolution and we all have the capacity for growth, wisdom and understanding. It is a matter of never giving up mentally, no matter what seeming obstacles appear in our paths. The solution is always there even before the apparent problem. Don't be either blind or deaf to it. What has worked for me is just to go to some quiet, private place and open my mind to an endless source of inspiration. It works! Our source never leaves us. Let all the good pour in. If you have never tried it, try it now. If you already know of this way of life, use it constantly. We are confronted with a myriad of distractions every day and need to be guided back to "the good life" wherein lies our true joy. Joy to me is the capacity to love and be loved. The ME that I am and the YOU that you are is physically healthy, eternally youthful, creative, altruistic, energetic, spiritually motivated, mentally alert, good humored, spontaneously funny, demonstrative in affection, forgiving in nature, kind in manner, articulate in communicating, graceful in conduct, moral and ethical in transactions, free of resentment or envy or jealousy or frustration, industrious in our work, living life with courage and faith. The WE that we are needs reminding that WE are all that We are...so let's be reminded together every day."

Here's another excerpt from the same book: Page 15 "We were put on this earth, not to suffer or feel unworthy of happiness, but to the contrary...We are here to be all that we can be to ourselves and to the rest of the world. We cannot dwell within ourselves and brood and fill ourselves with self-pity, fear, apathy and resentment. Be glad that you have this wonderful opportunity to be you...and to find out Who and What YOU really are. Joy is the reward. A joyful person is an achiever, a doer, a creator, a receiver of all good things. Joy attracts Joy.

"Only a true neurotic is happy with ill health, whether physical or emotional. They don't understand they have a choice. Depression causes most illness...Happiness heals all ills. You can be a happy, healthy person when you have taken good care of yourself and then turned your attention to the world around you. Get involved. Give of yourself. Inspire others to do the same. Know that you have all the intelligence and energy you will ever need to accomplish anything that you have to do. Meditate and be silent and gather this knowledge that is hovering all about you just waiting for you to grab hold. Be receptive in your attitude. The proper attitude is always necessary to receive inspiration.

"You are part of one complete whole of humanity. All beings have common emotions such as love, hate, fear, anger...So why would you decide that you are worse or better than anyone else. Meet on a common ground with the rest of humanity."

CAUSE & EFFECT

FETUS

Where does thought begin...When does thought begin...Why does thought begin???? What does thought cause? We are now going to begin to destroy the myths that are destroying the human race. These myths have been perpetuated by parents, grandparents, and other well-intentioned "elders" as well as the medical profession in its primitive state and other so-called authorities still living in the unenlightened state and those of the clergy who do not yet understand where true wisdom comes from. Is there anyone I have not yet offended? Do not take offense! No matter how difficult it is to release erroneous beliefs, it must be done if the human race is to survive, thrive and create a better humanity and planet. We are in Harm's Way...There is a Real and Present Danger. Time is of the essence. Resistance to enlightenment could not only slow up the process of forming a better life, but also could destroy that which we have developed so far...the good that is.

The babe in the womb is aware of the sounds of the world. What information are you feeding it? Does it hear things like: predisposed to, heredity, imperfect genes, weaknesses, fears, no gain without pain, angry words, shouting, excessive decibels, discouraging remarks, hostility, jealousy, meanness, hopelessness, and all other thoughts that would make the child afraid to come out of the womb to face such a horrible world? Think on this: A babe hearing only beautiful sounds, pleasant words, encouraging statements, laughter, talk of health and well being of vitality and creativity (and allowing that the mother does not take drugs, including alcohol and nicotine and caffeine and the illegal horrors, plus medicines not for pregnant women). Allowing for all this...perhaps labor pains will be a thing of the past because of easy dilation and smooth delivery. It is certainly worth trying! Give the kid a break will you and make life easier for you. When that babe has heard such good "stuff" it will come sliding out as was intended by Divine Mind.

INFANCY

Now the babe is out of the womb...into the light...but if it is not the light of wisdom, it may only blind him/her. What a tremendous responsibility for parents to impart this wisdom to the infant. What can they use as guidance? Sadly the human has not yet acquired this wisdom itself to pass on to the offspring. I suggest that after reading of how the babe is aware of the world as it hears it from the womb, you are now somewhat prepared to be on guard against filling the receptive mind of the infant with negative, limiting and harmful ideas.

No matter what fears and myths you were raised with, you must not pass these onto the young ones. Can we say often and loud enough that YOU ARE NOT A SLAVE TO HEREDITY! YOU ARE NOT A VICTIM OF YOUR GENES! NATURAL CHANGES AND DEVELOPMENTS OF THE BODY ARE NOT DISEASES! PAIN IS NOT A NATURAL STATE. WE DO NOT HAVE TO CARRY THE BURDEN OF 'OLD WIVES TALES' REGARDING NATURAL FUNCTIONS OF THE BODY. You must free your mind of these erroneous thoughts and beliefs so that you do not become the progenitor of harmful ideas.

TEACH SIBLING LOVE TO
AVOID SIBLING RIVALRY.

What I am stating here is not a new discovery. This wisdom has been available to humans for many centuries and for the past few decades quite widely published and lectured on. For some unfathomable reason, the human race has been resisting the very knowledge that can keep it operating on an optimum plane. Continued good health, youthfulness, vitality, creativity, beauty of thought and deed, capacity to love and understand, ability to perform good and great works, develop talents, enjoy the beauty of your world and learn how to protect it... all this and more... the bliss of life...is the mission of the human race. BUT in order to fulfill your mission you must stop resisting the enlightenment that is yours for the taking.

If you do not learn, you will perpetuate the ills of the human race and pass on to your beloved infants the fears and limitations that have crippled and pained and plagued the human race for generations. It has to dawn upon the mind of the adult human that there is a better way to think, believe and experience life so that you may teach this higher way to your children.

No one, infant or adult, need ever "catch" what is going around. No one need inherit "bad" genes. No one needs to expect to deteriorate with the years. At 70 I am healthier and stronger and more vitally alive than I have ever been and I have led a busy active life...having overcome terrible ills (no one told me that I did not have to have them...hence this manual so that others do not have to suffer needlessly). Do not let this effort of mine be in vain... It is being Divinely dictated for truth.

Protect your infant from loud noises, continuous loud music and other sounds that may impair the child's hearing. NEVER SMOKE IN THE SAME ROOM WITH A CHILD. The child needs fresh air, needs to be kept clean, well fed and embraced often. AND you must repeatedly tell the child you love her/him. Protect your child from over exposure to sun, (skin and eyes especially.) Unlike the machines and vehicles that your other manuals advise how to operate...the human is a work in progress and what you are doing is actually building a human body and mind.

We are the result of everything we have ever heard, seen, breathed in, smelled and thought...and eaten & drunk. We are the result of everything we have ever done to our bodies including a lack of exercise or too much strain on the body. It is obvious, therefore, that from the word "go" we must do right by the human "machine" we are creating.

It is at this stage that the adults must display good manners and appropriate behavior so that the child may have good role models. Yes, even as infants, the humans are absorbing and retaining and recalling everything going on around them. Be aware of this! You are being observed and heard. Is this how you want your children to behave? THINK!

CHILDHOOD

Oh, poor beleaguered, bewildered, besieged and bedazzled child. "IT" is coming at you from all directions. IT contradicts itself, confuses and confounds. IT is all so exasperating and frustrating. IT is all the "stuff" you hear from unenlightened elders, siblings and peers. IT consists of every fear, superstition, prejudice, resentment, anxiety, hostility, belief, bad judgment, foolishness, myth, and fairy tale that each one passes on to you. You must be wise enough and brave enough to break the chain of ignorance. Don't worry... I'll help you. You are in such an important phase of human development that this manual could be the "stuff" that <u>must</u> do it for you. An Owner's Manual to let you know what is right for a healthy mind and body...as opposed to the "bad stuff" that has messed up so much of your generation. Go argue with that! If you don't know that huge numbers of children get off to such a bad start that they remain sick of mind and body through adulthood, here are some sobering truths. Every toxin you inhale, ingest or come in contact with can and usually does have very damaging effects on you both physically and mentally. Excessive sound (including the most abusive in the form of music (?) with or without the use of earphones) not only impairs your hearing but also upsets your entire nervous system (very bad damage that gets worse as you get older). You may be doing such harm to yourself that you may never have a healthy and satisfying adulthood. I KID YOU NOT! There are so many adults on this planet right now that have difficulty breathing, hearing, studying, working, walking, even talking, playing, reading, enjoying sports and the arts... just because they either did some or all of the really stupid things that they thought were "cool" at the time. Poor fools...but I feel so sorry for them. A lot of these people were warned one way or another about the dangers of some of the substances or acts, but they had the ridiculous idea that they were invulnerable... IT CAN'T HAPPEN TO ME! Yeah, right!

Hey, kids, this is no joke! The joke could be on you, but you won't be laughing. In plain English...Don't smoke ANYTHING (it really does stink)...Don't try to acquire a taste for alcoholic beverages (and it does take time because liquor tastes awful). Either of these alone will wreck your mind and body...but wait...there is more...Stop eating junk food, drinking anything with caffeine in it, filling yourself with fatty foods...You don't want to grow up fat, nervous and with clogged arteries... Believe me... YOU DON'T WANT ALL THAT! GET SMART and breath the cleanest air you can find. Drink plenty of pure water. Get lots of good exercise. Sleep at least 7-8 hours a night. Keep your body clean. Take good care of your teeth and gums. Shampoo your hair often. Get involved with healthful activities. Be eager to get a good education. Learn from great books. Use your mind to set high ideals and goals. Strive for excellence. No one is perfect, but we can be excellent in some things. You are very important, unique and loved. Know that!

You may hear people express dislike or even hatred for some complete race, or religion, or ethnic heritage. DO NOT LET THOSE IDEAS ENTER YOUR THOUGHT PROCESSES! IT IS SICK AND IGNORANT BEYOND COMPREHENSION! PEOPLE WHO EXPRESS AND EVEN DEMONSTRATE HATRED OF A COMPLETE RACE, RELIGION OR ETHNICITY ARE OF SUCH LOW CONSCIOUSNESS BECAUSE THEY WERE TAUGHT BY HUMANS JUST AS IGNORANT. This is not a chain of thought that can continue if the human race is to operate on a sane level.

YOU ARE THE PERSON WHO CAN START THE HUMAN RACE ON AN ASCENSION TO HIGH CONSCIOUSNESS. DO NOT BELIEVE IN ANY RACE SUPERIORITY, RELIGIOUS SUPERIORITY, OR ETHNIC SUPERIORITY. IT IS ABSOLUTELY FALSE INFORMATION. EACH INDIVIDUAL IS RESPONSIBLE FOR HIS/HER OWN BEHAVIOR. WEIGH YOUR THOUGHTS, WORDS AND ACTIONS AGAINST THE HIGHEST IDEALS AND SEE HOW YOU MEASURE UP. IF YOU ARE HARBORING ANY FEELINGS OF PREJUDICE BASED ON ANY TEACHING YOU MAY HAVE RECEIVED, KNOW NOW AND FOREVER THAT THIS IS A SICKNESS AND YOU WANT TO HAVE A HEALTHY MIND. If ignorance is the cause, then enlightenment is the cure. Learn about other people... their religion, their culture, their history and their true nature. Consider people one at a time. Do not bunch people together and make a blanket assumption. That is foolishness. Remember we do not want humans to be fools! Wisdom will correct all our ignorant words and actions. SEEK WISDOM! Will you recognize it when you see or hear it? Here is a clue...Wisdom knows no hatred. Wisdom knows no violence. Wisdom means no harm to anyone. Wisdom brings the right thought, words and action to any situation causing the right and proper outcome of any situation.

Right Thought =   Wisdom
Right Words =   Wisdom of Expression
Right Feelings =   Wisdom of Communication
Right Action =   Wisdom of Outcome

Try it; you will like it. Wisdom brings the courage to do the right things...that harm no one, including yourself.

SCHOOL: Develop in yourself the eagerness to learn all the necessary subjects including language, history, geography, the humanities, mathematics, science, writing, reading, art, music, physical education, and hygiene. Have respect for your teachers. Develop concepts; keep your mind alert. HAVE QUIET THOUGHTFUL PERIODS.

YOUNG ADULT

Ah...Let me catch you quickly before you are set so deeply into the cement of erroneous thinking and doing that it will take extra chipping away to get to the glorious being you are. You think I exaggerate? Oh if you only knew. But then you may know when you read on...

What is a glorious being? One who manifests all the potential that was given as a gift. Each has a different gift. As this wondrous unique being, it is up to you to examine your inclinations towards any and all abilities, talents and all good works.

Education does not end with graduation from any formal structure, but increases with every book we read, every lecture we attend, every extra class we take. Education increases by observing and researching. Hunger for learning must never cease. Open up to the wisdom of those who have taken the time and thought to explore more than archaic beliefs. Read books written by those on the cutting edge of advanced thinking. I am referring to Dr. Deepak Chopra, Dr. Andrew Weil, Dr. Herbert Benson, Dr. Abraham Maslow, Dr. Christiane Northrup (See Bibliography). Such enrichment of the mind will open doors to better health, slower aging, freedom from destructive beliefs of heredity, of degeneration, of "being predisposed to", of limitation, (Please refer to the chapter on myths and misinformation). With a gloriously healthy and fit body and a mind so enriched, you are prepared for your very important part in the evolution of the human race and the salvation of the planet. Chances are you did not know that is your mission. Well now you know it is. Who were you going to leave it to? To chance? Eeegads, what have you been thinking? Wake up you budding creature and realize your full potential. Waste not, Want not. Never be dismayed or discouraged. Things may not proceed according to your hasty heart, but "Take one day at a time and make it a masterpiece." (A quotation I picked up somewhere) and you may accumulate a complete gallery of masterpieces.

Develop a sense of humor. Always look for a light side. Snoopy has said, "Remember there is no problem so large that we cannot walk away from it." I also take wisdom wherever I find it. With regard to so-called problems, the solution is always right within them. Now what does that all mean? You don't really walk away from a so-called problem. You look at it from another angle. Shed more light on the subject. Stop and be quiet and let wisdom creep in. Aha...you will say, "Why didn't I think of that." If you get too engrossed with problems, you lose sight of proper solutions. The solution must always be one that does not harm you or anyone else (or their possessions) or be unethical or immoral...or harm the environment... or undo any good work that has been done. What is left is the perfect answer to any problem. Fairness, justice, patience, flexibility, innovativeness, ingenuity, creativity, far-sightedness, generosity, confidence and trust make up the right solutions.

You are forming new relationships in your work place, in your institutions of higher learning, social gatherings, in club events, etc. and you will encounter many views and personalities, some of which may be counterproductive to your evolvement as your "highest self". Please remember through all of these experiences that you can decide whether to be distracted and allow yourself to be diminished, or you can hold fast to your ideals and enlarge your true self.

The latter choice is the one that leads to fulfillment and bliss. It is a gift to have a good mind, clear and unfettered by "altered states." It is a gift to have a strong, healthy body that is not ravaged by toxins and abuse of any sort. It is a blessing to have loved ones in our life to treat with affection, respect and consideration. It is a privilege to use our talents and intelligence and wisdom for the good of humanity and our environment. What rich, rewarding lives we are preparing ourselves for. What vitality it brings to us to know we can contribute our best. It makes us eager to discover what more we are capable of. Catch the good energy that is encircling our planet... the energy that combines with the true wisdom to make wondrous changes for the betterment of life on earth. **YOU ARE AN IMPORTANT PERSON IN THIS TRANSFORMATION!** Do not be afraid to take on your portion of the responsibility. It will never be more than you can handle. If one day at a time seems too much, try one hour at a time. Just keep on. It is such joy to see the universe cooperate with us when we do our share.

ADULT

Maturing but not yet middle aged: This is the "top form" time if you have been eating properly, exercising enough and correctly, avoiding toxins in any form, breathing clean air, drinking pure water, protecting yourself (skin and eyes) from over exposure to sunlight, keeping your teeth and gums healthy, observing proper hygiene, getting enough sleep and rest, protecting your ears from excessive decibels and pursuing uplifting activities.

IF NOT, START IMMEDIATELY! YOU CAN REPAIR YOURSELF!

Keep an open mind about the human's ability to undo the damage to itself. Unlike the machines for which we have operating manuals, we have self-healing mechanisms, which we need to learn how to operate. Unlike machines that come from the factory already manufactured (perhaps just to assemble), we humans are doing most of the manufacturing of ourselves by ourselves. Did you know that? You are the product of your belief system. Let us draw from some ancient wisdom to know that "we receive in accordance with our beliefs". Probably no truer words were ever spoken or written. Next would be the great observation, "that which I have feared has come upon me"...because fear is a magnet, not because you were able to predict correctly. If you examine your thoughts very carefully, you will discover (perhaps to your amazement) that you are acting out these thoughts.

Since this is truth in action, think on this, "Thought produces effect." So first consider what effect you desire and think on that. I guess simplicity is too complicated for some human minds...but use the KISS principle...Keep it Simple Sweetheart...and see how easy it is. Don't muddy clear waters.

Our thoughts may be the beginning of all experience, but our emotions carry a lot of weight. Our various emotions have a corresponding effect on our well-being. Loving thoughts produce a chemical reaction in the body conducive to health. While thoughts of resentment and hostility produce chemical reactions that result in various physical ills such as arthritis, gallstones, ulcers, clogged arteries, heart problems, even cancer. Science has not discovered why that happens. It is depressing to think other than loving thoughts, so therefore, this depression causes a weakening or even shutting down of the immune system, which in turn allows the body to play host to illness. If you follow all this word-by-word you will understand how we actually cause our illness and affliction (including allergies, which are also emotionally induced) by our less than admirable thoughts and emotions. WELL! You may well say. How can I control every thought and emotion that is harmful to me? You don't have to. Just don't let those thoughts and emotions stay around for any length of time. As soon as possible, replace them with loving, forgiving, compassionate and peaceful ones. Start with thanking God (or higher self) for all of your many blessings. Dwell on your good fortune. Using the problem solving principles as explained in the chapter on "Young Adults", you too can reach all solutions joyfully.

So many people make excuses for older people doing and saying less than logical things, but I sincerely feel that if they had lived a healthier lifestyle, these "older" folk would not be in this sad state of affairs now. IT doesn't just happen! Aging is, as I have said before, not an illness... We can die in good health...when it is time to go...and not wither away in mind and body...and perhaps even soul. The people who allowed this to happen (and it was done in ignorance) needed to have an Owner's Manual to live by. May no future generation have to suffer this way... Amen.

NORMAL CHANGES

Both males and females go through their own various natural changes know as growth. It is never an "awkward age". It is nothing to feel "unnatural" about. It is never a "curse" for that natural function. "Change of Life" is a myth along with "mid-life Crises". Mankind has so maligned and misnamed so much of life experiences that they cannot know how much psychological and therefore how much physiological damage they have done (the one always precedes the other). Let us change all that with clarification and truth.

To pervert nature's intention, by distorting that which is necessary to develop as maturing humans, is one of the greatest travesties committed against the human race.

We are created to develop along very logical stages. All of which, when looked at with wisdom and understanding, make so much sense we can marvel at the great plan.

Let us take menopause for example. This, of course, is not an illness and therefore should not be seen and treated as such. All that truly happens is that the woman runs out of eggs! She at say 50 doesn't need them anymore, so nature in all Divine practicality rids her of them. Do women really want to go on having babies in their fifties??? Not if they are thinking clearly. So if they don't get rid of the eggs they could go on having babies ad infinitum! With such intelligence in the universe, how can we put a negative slant on so great a miracle! Now for the "title" put on this marvelous occurrence, women are to believe (inspired by some person of little understanding) they are going through "change of life". Oh dear...what a crock! Don't you believe that one for a nanosecond.

You are no less of a woman after you stop supplying eggs to be fertilized. That stage is not the final act to any play! You keep on living a normal life...playing, working, loving and making love. If you suffer in any way, it is because you have been conditioned by brainwashing that this is a bad thing. Wake up and don't let these ignorant beliefs control your well being ... I didn't and you don't have to either. I don't wear estrogen patches...what a crock. God knows what kind of hormones you are supposed to have and arranges it just the way it should be. Don't let your fears interfere with normal wonderful changes. It is your fears and bad conditioning that produce complications and hormone imbalance. Put your mind at peace and welcome all natural changes with joy and relief. You will see how well you feel in mind, body and emotions. Most all human problems come from superstitions, ignorance and fear...this is just one of them.

Note: Hey ladies...When the grocery store runs out of eggs, it doesn't get hot flashes....hmmmm.

MIDDLE AGE (SO CALLED)
-- REALLY, SPRINGTIME!

Depending on who is trying to convince you, motivated by their own purposes, this could be any where from 26 to 40. To me coming from my own experience and revelation, middle age is between 60 and 80. Although the pundit's latest figures state that we were built to last 120 years, I prefer to think of our years as seasons...40 years each. Up to age 40 we are springtime. The seeds are being planted, and the early blooms are visible. How we are nurtured during these years will have a profound effect on us. All the beliefs we attach ourselves to will affect our body, environment and experiences. Not to say that at any age we cannot do a 180-degree turn for the better; but the older we get, the more of a challenge it will seem. So during springtime years we need to surround ourselves with true wisdom that opens us up to fine ideals, high standards of morality and ethics. We can benefit greatly from the arts...listening to great music, reading great books, looking at great paintings, developing our own talents, getting out into nature (like walks along the beach or sitting among the trees in a park), breathing in clean air and enjoying the silence, learning to meditate (and in that quiet time learning to accept the inspiration that comes to us...then feeling the energy that comes to us to complete our tasks), using our body well with sensible, well-balanced exercise, learning to love more deeply and express that love, sharpening our minds so that we are alert. Dance, sing, play games (requiring physical or mental prowess), ...write poetry or prose. Build or sculpt or paint. Be involved with people of high purpose and good dispositions. Go sailing, traveling, motoring on a country lane. Know that health is your birthright and accept it.

We have been expressing repeatedly the need to free ourselves from belief in inheriting bad genes. We have explained how science (among the more enlightened) has come to realize that we are not a slave to heredity and "gene power"...that we can transform ourselves by our beliefs. Our hormones can and will do seemingly miraculous feats if we are of high enough consciousness to accept them. These are not words from weird sources even though they have been used inappropriately in some areas. What a shame that so much wisdom has been distorted for gain or attention. There really is such a thing as being of higher consciousness: Simply said, it means that once you are truly aware of the powers you have been given by "Divine Mind" and apply them to the benefit of all, you are of a higher consciousness. You know it when you do it. Springtime is such a wonderful time for a fresh start. Get the cobwebs out of your brain (attic) and do a clean sweep (otherwise known as spring cleaning) in the rest of your body. Summer is approaching and you want to be well prepared to live your life healthy and full of good energy to do even greater things.

SUMMERTIME -- FULL BLOOM

It stands to reason if until age 40 we are in springtime... that from 40 to...yes 80 we can enjoy summertime. Here is how. We have only to recognize that in living a healthy lifestyle (previously explained in this book) there need not be an acceptance of what heretofore has been thought to be an inescapable aging process...a process whereby we deteriorate or even fall apart. Throw out that picture immediately. Remember whatever pictures you keep in mind...will reproduce in kind. No matter how rapidly or badly anyone in your family has aged...no matter what illness or degenerative diseases they exhibited...YOU DO NOT HAVE TO BE A PART OF THAT PICTURE.

Please think about this...it is very important. No two people...no matter how closely related...have the same thoughts precisely in the same manner, picture, words or feelings. So since you are thinking independently, being the unique individual that you are, your thoughts, words and feelings are uniquely your own. <u>And these are the things that will reproduce (or manifest) themselves in your body...and life!</u>

It really is quite simple...Truth always is. You will receive in accordance with your beliefs. Living in a senior citizen building for three years plus some months, I see all around me the results of so much erroneous thinking. How do I know what their thinking is??? I asked them (Simple again). Their thoughts as expressed by the great majority simply put... "At our age you have got to expect to have these things happen; everyone has something wrong; so what...you have to accept the inevitable, etc." How terribly sad and exasperating! They spent spring and summer with poor diets, lack of exercise, lack of interests and worst of all, with erroneous thoughts...and I'm seeing and hearing the results of this tragedy of misguided minds destroying themselves. IT NEED NOT HAVE BEEN AND MUST NOT GO ON!

Where is it written that at a certain age you must lose your hearing...eyesight...sense of balance...taste, that your bones have to thin out, teeth and/or gums rot, hair fall out, body become bent over, mind become weak... memory fail...disposition become miserable...OH GOD... IS IT REALLY WRITTEN ANYWHERE???? Of course not! NOT BY ANY DIVINE HAND!

At 71 years of age now (yes I have been at this book for a couple of years) I am in excellent health and energy and remain creative and very active (belonging to a few dance groups) and still have none of the above-mentioned deteriorations. My mother at age 73 (when she passed away from old age) had many of the maladies and was a very aged woman...So much for inheriting genes. Get over it! DO RIGHT FOR AND BY YOURSELF!

SENIOR – AUTUMN: A CHANGE OF COLOR

I know the further I progress into this four seasons theory; the more difficult it will be to accept the glory of it all. But here goes. Anyone living today who has reached the age of 80 would probably not think of autumn as the season they are entering now...more likely they feel they have been in winter for sometime already. BUT in the future...for people in springtime now (to 40)...after reading this book...they will understand how at age 80 (after a summer 40-80), autumn is the next glorious stage. The colors start to change (figuratively speaking) and there may be a bit of a chill in the air...but it is an invigorating chill. You still have 40 more years of joy and productivity. (Oh, come on––get with the program!)

Even today there are people in their hundreds who are active and mentally alert. Imagine in the future when humans have learned to clean the air, water, food and earth how much better a setting is for long healthy lives. This is, of course, only if they recognize and use their "God Power".

For any atheists who happen to be reading this, call the power anything you like...but use it!

Don't just let things happen to you...be a creator... have a say in what you are becoming...in what you can do. Achieve...enjoy. Follow the EASY OUTLINES presented in this book and see and feel the wondrous changes in you...body and soul.

WINTER

If we follow through with the seasons you are now 120 years of age and beautiful...since you have taken part in your evolution and this is what you have pictured for yourself...your thoughts have manifested themselves into a magnificent... well-accomplished creature...that at last can rest on your laurels if you choose to.

HOWEVER...

It is still not mandatory to stop whatever you feel inspired to do... Let us keep an open mind.

NOW THINK ON THIS!

If you take the seasons and turn them into 30-year periods instead of 40, you have come into the world that science has accepted as realistic. How do you measure up on that scale? 30 years of springtime, summertime until 60, autumn until 90 and winter until 120 (Why act as though you are 70 at age 50, when you could be like 50 at 70! I did!). We don't want to live forever, but I plan to die in good health! Long life means nothing if not spent well. Live well and let all your years be good ones.

CLARIFICATION OF MYTHS AND MISINFORMATION THAT HAVE LED HUMANS ASTRAY

Because so much of the medical profession, science, society and religion, plus any other source of belief that is unenlightened, have been so instrumental in forming the mindset of humans; the human race has been aging at too rapid a rate than is intended for us; has taken normal changes in the body to be diseases, or at least an inconvenience if not a distressful situation; has lost its ability to recognize its own power to correct and/or heal afflictions; has limited itself in its capabilities to achieve great works of mind and body; has ignored the unity of mankind so that divisiveness has caused terrorism, crime, violence and the worst of all, war; has caused itself much grief and strife in intrapersonal and interpersonal relations; has lost sight of the power of love; has lost a close relationship with God!

AGING

As *we* have stated, advanced science has revealed that humans are created to last 120 years. That means all of our physical attributes were created to endure for that length of time. More and more humans presently are doing that but not as frequently as in ancient times when living to 110 and 120 with mind and body in tact was common. (The ancients had not had their minds polluted with all the pollutions of modern times and therefore could allow a truer nature to take its course). Through the ages from biblical to old history to newer history to now, various organized groups, individuals and so-called authorities have imposed their superstitions and erroneous beliefs on the minds of the susceptible public. They have planted unfavorable pictures of the human race at growing stages into the mind so that the human, keeping that picture in mind, becomes what is kept in mind. In other words..."Thoughts kept in mind reproduce in kind." You get or become what you expect from the programming your mind has accepted. The mind is so much more powerful than the majority of the human race can conceive of. We must become aware of what we produce. Thoughts or fears of being incapacitated; of losing our faculties; of inheriting diseases and afflictions from our parents or farther back; of being useless; of helplessness in anyway.... All contribute to the destruction of the body and mind. THEY are the cause of accelerated aging. Recognize truth when it is revealed to you here.

(Why else do you think this is being written...I could be out dancing instead of taking this time to impart the enlightenment that has come into my mind to be shared with you. Use this valuable time).

HEREDITY

You may have heard the woman on TV when she explained that she had both of her healthy breasts removed because there was a history of breast cancer in her family. And more recently you may have heard one of TV's favorite MD's say that if a woman has a history of ovarian cancer in her family, she should have her ovaries removed after child-bearing years. The horrifying theories are still persisting because medical science is still not aware of true cause and effect. THE FEAR OF INHERITING CANCER IS A MAGNET THAT ATTRACTS IT! OUR BELIEFS ARE SO POWERFUL THEY CAN TRANSFORM HEALTHY TISSUE INTO MALIGNANT TISSUE! THE POWER OF SUGGESTION CAN CONTROL THE HUMAN MIND SO THAT IT OBEYS LIKE A THOUGHTLESS ROBOT! Cancer anywhere is exacerbated by resentment, severe depression and despair. The malignancy is the result of erroneous thinking.

Again...I repeat...you do not have to be a slave to heredity. Choose in your own uniqueness to be healthy in every respect...whether mentally, emotionally or physically. We are not carbon copies of anyone...no matter how closely related.

Every family has some history of some ailment and if we insist on believing that it has to be repeated we are defeating the glorious gift of regeneration and healing that has been granted to us by virtue of being born. I know with the medical profession so stuck in archaic training, it is difficult to rise above such ignorance, but we have to break away from old harmful and limiting ideas that are crippling the mind and body of us humans. Be yourself, know yourself, trust yourself and God. Every molecule of your body is solely yours, not some relatives. What do you want to experience? If it is perfect health, then break away from thoughts of inheriting bad genes!

GENE POWER

Earlier I mentioned the book THE WISDOM OF THE BODY by Sherwin Nuland, M.D., a renowned surgeon. Although the book is written brilliantly in precise medical and scientific form, it may be difficult for the average lay person to follow, and I would not want the seemingly miraculous ideas presented to be passed over for lack of understanding...So I would like to express my understanding of this great work as it pertains to this subject. I mentioned "gene expression" as one of his magnificent descriptions, which tells of activators and repressors of genes through our hormones. He also explains that we are malleable creatures able to mold ourselves. "We are greater than the sum of our biological parts". That greatness is our human spirit. It can overcome...override, cancel out the dark, erroneous thoughts and suggestions (yes, and even dire predictions that are delivered by the cock-sure scientific yet unenlightened world) and let in the light of wisdom...the wisdom that allows us to supplant the errors with truth!

By now you know that I choose to use various creative ways to get an idea across. In giving a lecture many years ago, I heard myself saying, "You have heard of designer jeans. Well I believe we can all be "designers of genes". Designer genes of another nature. I still believe that is true, and now, of course, we know how to do it. Using our hormones as repressors or activators of our genes. Our hormones respond to our thoughts and emotions.

Specifically, we can think of a gene that is in our family tree and decide that it is not appropriate for us. We can feel very deeply that we can be free of any undesirable gene. These thoughts and feelings produce the hormones that repress this unwanted gene.

As in the case of any physical phenomenon when genes do not always take the course expected, it is because some deep emotion on our part has intervened. As Dr. Chopra has stated that "nothing holds more power over the body than the beliefs of the mind," we can apply this here along with our emotions which have their seed in thought. KNOW HOW POWERFUL YOUR MIND IS! USE THAT POWER FOR GOOD!

Every day take time to examine your thoughts. At any age or physical condition know that you are still in control and are the authority and, therefore, can make changes for the better. Every cell in our body is changing every moment and this change is affected by thoughts... beliefs...convictions and imagination. Nothing in our bodies remains unchanging, so surely you can grasp the idea that WE have some responsibility and power to make changes that we prefer. YOU DO HAVE A SAY... AND THE CORRESPONDING RESPONSE WILL MANIFEST ITSELF!

This is not a fairy tale...And certainly not one of those destructive myths that people love to hold onto to their great disadvantage. This is not wishful thinking or wild speculation. It is the reality that so much of the human race thinks is too good to be true...when truth is so much greater and more wonderful than even this.

What miracles are you stopping from happening in your mind, body and life?

A miracle is the unexpected outcome of a seeming condition...AND WE ARE **THE MIRACLE WORKERS**! Get your mind and emotions in proper mode to perform and accept the miracles. Negative thinking (dark thoughts) and unwillingness to learn are the big obstacles in achieving the desired results. Fear is the darkest thought and attracts to it the thing that is feared. Get rid of the fear by replacing it with faith and you will get rid of bad genes and all the damage they can do. How much clearer do you need to have this said.

MID-LIFE CRISIS

I wonder what nerd thought that one up. It is all in the mind. If you use your mind constructively, healthfully, creatively (creativity in the sense of creating for good and beauty) and lovingly all through your growth periods, you will reach no mid-life crisis. Because through the years you have been fulfilling your dearest dreams, been accomplishing your goals one at a time, been loving to the greatest extent of your being, been planning new and even greater accomplishments and taking the steps to achieve them, seeing and enjoying each success...all is in order... and there is no crisis at any age... I promise you!

ACHIEVING GOALS

Whose dream are you living out? Yours or your parents, or grandparents, or teachers or clergy, friends, spouse, who.??? Are those aspirations really yours? How are you going to reach your goals if you don't really know what they are?? Know yourself. Examine your talents and abilities. Recognize your visions for your self. What do you see yourself accomplishing? Visualize and take all steps necessary to attain your goals. Never listen to "Nay Sayers"...those people who try to discourage you. They don't have your vision, don't realize your potential. They try to impose their limited thinking on you. Break free from such unenlightened influences. Use your own wisdom and do persevere.

Get the proper education and training. The world is full of sources of wisdom. Latch onto all the marvelous inspiration that is hovering all around you...waiting for you to accept it. Feel not only the inspiration, but also the energy to accomplish that which you have been inspired to do.

How often through the years I was told. "You can't do that," by those who did not have my vision or energy...and if I had listened to them or believed them...I would not have accomplished those things that have given me the greatest sense of achievement and pleasure. Thank God I listened to a higher calling. It is the still small voice, the divine nudge, the being led down the right paths...it is intuition! (Which is covered in depth later in this book).

FUTURE GOALS

We have not even scratched the surface of the human/ divine potential. Think of the human race free of limiting ideas of illness and early aging; free of being afflicted with heretofore believed to be "inherited" ills; free of being susceptible to anything "going around"; free of feeling unworthy to do great works, ... this is the freedom that is ours for the taking right now, but it is up to each of us to be in full realization of this truth.

The future is beginning everyday and our choices will have a profound effect on the ascension of mankind or its destruction. The higher the thinking...the higher the ascension. If we persist in limited thinking we will put the human race in a stagnating position where we keep repeating the horrors of all the woes of the human race. You are in the race!!!

You do not only own yourself, but an important part of the big picture. You have your special part to fill. You are completely responsible for your thoughts, words and actions. You have serious decisions to make about these thoughts, words and actions. Are you going to hang back with outrageous theories and myths that are destroying you??? Or are you going to free your Divine mind to inspire you to higher thinking, speech and deeds.

Ah the day when doctors no longer diagnose incorrectly and prescribe dangerously for ailments they not only don't understand but also cannot fathom the cause thereof. It is sad that this should be one of the most exasperating aspects of human existence...but without good health, it is not possible to achieve all the great works that need to be done...

Now to take on the environment: "Polluted minds produce pollution." Minds that think only of profit and not the consequences of their actions are producing unbreathable air, undrinkable water, inedible food and harmful products of every description. An advanced mind would discover ways to clean up the planet and enrich all of our lives with the true goodness of the earth. An advanced mind would have the courage to be so innovative that even industries that exist only for profit regardless of their harmful effects on people and plants would see the light of the benefit of change for them and all involved. We changed from horse and buggy to the polluting vehicles of today without thought to health. It was called progress. Now true progress will be...to have vehicles that DO NOT POLLUTE! It can and will be done. We cannot continue on this way. Higher consciousness must prevail!

Let us take on education. I'm certain that I was not the only person who noticed as far back as 30 years ago that students were getting out of school unable to spell or do math, and that about 20 years ago teachers started to sound and look like hoodlums off the street. No dignity or decorum could be attributed to them and they were presenting themselves (and being hired) as role models for so much of the younger generation. Children receive "education" from many sources...home, school, religious institutions, the streets...but so much of their time is actually in a school that it is inexcusable to have let that institution deteriorate to the mess it is in now. I will never understand why it takes so long for the public to be aware of the problems and then take even longer to solve them. Of course teachers must be tested not only to see if they know their subject well enough, but also to see if they know how to impart that knowledge. They must also be able to hold discipline and order in the classroom. Their attire and conduct must be appropriate and they should be able to inspire their charges with high standards of conduct. If we think we are doing the world a favor by being "soft" on discipline and allowing teachers and students to get by on such a low level of achievement, we have another think coming. Without good education we are doomed!

We can pretend we do not understand how all the ills of our world came into being, but to face them honestly we must have the courage to admit to apathy, laziness, a turning away from any problem whether personal or global, a shirking of our responsibilities, a contributing to those problems ourselves, a disregard for our own well-being and certainly for the well-being of others by harmful acts or carelessness, making excuses for our behavior or lack of action, thinking if we just don't pay attention to "it", it will just go away, or all of the above!

Well, folks, "all of the above" just won't do. What will it take to make you realize it. Where in this world are you going to go to escape it? Hey, wake up, there is no place. This is it! And YOU are it.

Start by shaping yourself up, mind, emotions, body and soul. How can you do any good for you or the world if you are a mess? A chain is only as strong as its weakest link, so as a link in the chain of humanity you must be strong. Strength comes from inner courage, integrity, faith and wisdom. Help yourself to large portions; it is yours for free and the asking and taking. Take, take and give, give. Only through this exchange done universally, can we ascend according to the Great Plan.

DIVISIVENESS

Oh what a global yet very personal travesty this subject is. To correct this erroneous thinking and all the misinformation that has been accepted as truth will require every one of us to be cleansed of all prejudice and hatred. But before we can do that we must be reeducated. Nature abhors a vacuum so if we take away something that has filled the minds and hearts of so much of the human race such as all this unreasonable hatred, intolerance and prejudice, we must have ready all of the understanding, love and compassion that must replace them.

We are all God's beloved children and in Divine eyes there is no difference at all. Divisiveness is a humanly contrived device born out of ignorance and fear. It is born out of the insecurity of a race of beings that do not know their own divinity and in that ignorance established organizations and institutions to separate themselves from others who also felt so insecure and built other institutions to enhance their image.

And so it continued, new religion after old and those being split and in contention with each other. Each wanting to feel superior to the other, more important, and using disparaging remarks against each other so that the people in any sect had to feel animosity towards the other.

Religion is and has been one of the greatest causes of divisiveness, but language, culture, color, dress, politics, economics and anything that any human could find to criticize about another has added to all the separateness of beings that were meant to unite in a higher evolution of earthlings.

So if we can never all have the same religion, the same color skin, enjoy the same cultural traditions, speak the same language, dress the same, have the same amount of riches, live in the same environment, SO WHAT? We do not have to have any of those things in common to be able to be kind, compassionate and considerate. (Ah, so that is what she is talking about, she just wants us to be kind to each other, aha!)

If it has not dawned on you by now that the world requires wisdom for true happiness and fulfillment, you have not been paying attention. Wash away ignorance, Come up with a clean and higher consciousness. Now what do you have?...that wonderful receptacle ready to be filled with enlightenment.

Note to Religionists: All religions must believe, talk, act, write and preach LOVE! NO MORE DIVISIVENESS! No feelings of superiority, of specialness, or condemnation of others can continue. The human race cannot endure any longer such abominations.

THE POWER OF LOVE

By now the word synergy is widely known and understood. With synchronized energy we can do such great works of humanity that love could be the only motivating force on the planet. Here is the plan: since thoughts kept in mind reproduce in kind; we must each appoint ourself a committee of one to keep thoughts loving. Now that combined with the next person who is doing the same thing causes a greater power than the sum of its parts. In other words, instead of 1+1=2, with synergy 1+1=a powerful force. A force of love. I say it is well worth trying. Remember we are not just building a human body, but a soul as well. The soul is a composite of all our thoughts and requires love to survive. Surely you feel that. There is no greater power in the universe. For me, God is love and God is the only power I turn to. Bliss is in your soul, feel it, let it comfort and caress you.

We must make people aware, and only through love, of all our common bonds, concentrating on the unifying forces. This unity can only be accomplished through the power of love. Anything else, any other method, will fail.

RELATIONSHIP WITH GOD

During the past decade the medical world has discovered that people who are suffering from illness recover more rapidly and more often if they have some kind of faith. That is not surprising to those of us who have recovered from serious illness through the activity of God in our mind and body. The pity is that so much of the human race still remains ignorant of this marvelous unchanging truth. The mind of mankind can be the most stubborn, dogmatic, self-destructive and hindering force in the universe.

If an elixir were offered to the human race for thousands of dollars made up by some pharmaceutical company to heal all ills, no matter how expensive it would be, there would be a huge demand for it; but offered for free, yours in the form of faith, it would be rejected, and the irony of it all is that faith works better than most drugs, without the terrible side effects. "Be you transformed by the renewing of your mind". You see I am very eclectic in my sources of wisdom. Although some religions do not recognize a Divine Being, the philosophy of one religion is divine in its teaching of right attitude, right thinking, right speech and right action. Releasing all low thought, speech and action and accepting only the highest brings us into a close relationship with God. We need this relationship to be centered in wisdom and to receive inspiration. We cannot rely on our intellect for this. It is peace and guidance beyond human capabilities. The healing is the healing of the soul.

RELATIONSHIP WITH HUMANS

How often we hear parents complaining that their children are unruly and won't listen to their words of "wisdom". The parents seem to be at a loss in trying to discipline children of all ages and especially "teenagers". When we go out into the world of employment we have had to be schooled and trained to hold a position and perform it well. The most important "job" humans will ever have is to be a parent. Where is the training for that? Men and women are expected to know "instinctively" how to raise a child. How ridiculous! Chances are these "new" parents did not like or approve of the way they were raised by their parents. So where are the role models? Parents cannot expect to raise well-adjusted children if they are not very well adjusted themselves. If parents are displaying unethical and/or immoral behavior, the children will be conditioned accordingly. If the children have some good input from other sources, they may be able to overcome past errors. BUT DON'T RELY ON THAT! Training begins in the home. That responsibility must be accepted. If parents are users of illegal drugs (the damage from which has not been stressed enough), the children will believe this is accepted behavior. If parents are lazy, dishonest and undependable, the children may emulate this lifestyle to their detriment. Children are not born with the knowledge of right and wrong. They depend on their parents to teach them. If this is your "job" be sure you are up to high standards of teaching.

So you were not raised "to perfection", but let us not keep dwelling on that. Stop the blame game and take a good look at yourself, whether parent, child of any age, adult of any age (and that goes for seniors too) and start shaping up now.

Whom are you letting influence you? Peers can be the most destructive or helpful influence depending on whether they understand right from wrong, good from bad, healthful from harmful, etc. If you are depending on just your peers to guide you, you may be carrying around a lot of erroneous thinking.

You have heard of the blind leading the blind. Well, it does not work well. Someone has to see the light. And here is the light. Read over the <u>Easy Outline</u> pages and try to follow all the <u>do's</u> and let go of the <u>don'ts</u>. Chances are you will be healthier, happier and get along with people a whole lot better.

Whether the relationship is Parent-Child, Parent-Parent, Peers, Spouse-Spouse, Employer-employee, Friend-Friend, Neighbors, fellow employees, Tenant-Management, Traveling companions, you name it, your behavior consisting of integrity, honesty, compassion, understanding and enlightenment will improve all situations.

INTUITION

This very real and most important gift is given to all. Be aware that there is such a thing. It is in everyone.

Learn to recognize it. Be aware of its presence. Notice the messages your being is receiving from this Divine source.

Learn to accept and act on your intuitive powers. God communicates with us through our intuition.

What is it?? It has been called that "gut feeling"; "something told me'" "an unexplainable knowing"; "an idea that came from nowhere" (after meditation); "a deep understanding of what is right"; "a realization that you have a mission to perform"...and what it all adds up to... is that we do have Divine Guidance and it speaks to us through our intuition.

Our attention in keeping open the line of direct communication with this Higher Wisdom should have a very high priority in our everyday activity...from the smallest task to our most pressing responsibility. There is always a better way, a more beautiful behavior, a more beneficial result and a more gracious attitude. All of this comes to us if we accept the Divine Guidance that comes through our intuition.

Strange that this precious gift is so ignored by so many: Those who are always so sure that they are always right, no matter who they hurt, even themselves; Those who are so limited in their thinking that they will not allow themselves to be open to this great enlightenment; Those who dogmatically stick to their robot-like behavior that does not allow for the flexibility necessary for advancement; and other skeptics who choose to remain in the dark ages...do not realize they are obstacles on the highway to the ascension of the human race, but they are!

They are the people who seem to be in the wrong place at the wrong time, doing the wrong thing, causing much trouble and pain. They act out of thoughtlessness and ignorance, and sometimes out of selfishness and greed. They have ignored the gift of intuition to the point of being numb to all Divine Guidance. Do not be a part of this group of humans who cause so much strife and suffering in the world. Now that you know how to overcome such behavior, or avoid it to begin with, do go into the silence and get in touch with your own intuition. Your soul will sing and dance with joy, and it loves to do that. You are on your way to blissful living!

EXERCISE

Although it has been claimed that walking is all the exercise you need to keep physically fit, and it also has been claimed that swimming is the best exercise, I have found that the best, well balanced, all inclusive exercise is calisthenics.

If push-ups and sit-ups are too strenuous to do, there are many movements that not only are easy to do, but also very enjoyable. At 71, I find that working out with 2 lb. weights (mine are cushioned with foam covers) with simple movements that involve every part from head to toe (literally) done to lively music is invigorating and keeps me flexible and not subject to a lot of aches and pains, nor rigidness and deterioration.

I cannot stress the importance of exercise enough. Most of the problems of people are due to a lack of exercise. If you know any senior citizens who are very disabled, you can probably trace their ailments to a lack of proper exercise. I see hundreds of seniors and the shape they are in is deplorable.

If you don't want to spend your "golden" years needing an aid to help you along with either a cane or more likely a walker, get busy with starting a wise and healthful exercise regimen. TODAY isn't too soon.

A suggestion: If you don't like to exercise alone, or don't know how to begin, why not join a dance class. Dancing is one of the most beneficial ways to get the body moving. OR if you join a gym, make sure the exercises are right for you. If you don't like the jumping up and down stuff (I dislike it) find a teacher whose style fits yours.

If you want to exercise in private, get a book or video on the subject. The instructions are very easy to follow and usually are categorized as easy, moderate and advanced.

Drink plenty of water before, during and after exercise.

Dress comfortably with clothes that do not bind or chafe. Wear proper footwear.

If you need to hold on to a bar or chair for balance for some exercises (like leg kicks) make sure they are secure. Use good judgment in all you do to and for your body. Get advice from a trainer if you need to.

ALLERGIES

The definition in the dictionary is "a hypersensitivity to a specific substance such as food, pollen, dust, etc., or condition such as heat or cold, which in similar amounts, is harmless to most people. It is manifested in a physiological disorder".

What is left out is the cause of such hypersensitivity. Since everything begins in thought and subsequently emotions, the person suffering from such condition must very carefully, thoroughly and honestly examine their thoughts and feelings.

My observations, having lived in three states (New York, Arizona and California) and Greece have shown a definite connection between the mental and emotional state of the person and the severity and even the existence of an allergy to natural substances indigenous to this planet.

The more overwrought, insecure, hostile, frustrated, unhappy and/or lonely the person, the more severe the allergy was manifested. In Arizona the problem was further exacerbated by living in enclosed air conditioned environments where the air is constantly recycled no matter how bad it is and probably more important, the person has isolated himself from natural air to the point where it is foreign to him and a reaction is realized upon being exposed to what ordinarily would be good air, to most people.

Very often a person having a reaction to tobacco smoke or vehicle exhaust is wrongly labeled as having an allergy. That is like saying a person is allergic to poison. The reaction (coughing, headache, throat irritation, burning eyes, etc) is our bodies very wisely warning us that we are in danger. This kind of "sensitivity" can save our lives.

BUT being sensitive to things in their natural state when no toxins are involved is a sign that this person must change their thinking. If you are one of the sufferers, please know that you and you alone can rid yourself of this most annoying and debilitating affliction. Here is how: Get rid of every hurt you are carrying around (the person who hurt you has either forgotten it or never realized he hurt you to begin with), stop being angry with anyone or anything (what good does it do)? Meditate and feel at peace with everyone and the world in general, enjoy your own company, develop a sense of humor, find enjoyable things to do, be demonstrative in your affection, never feel rejected or belittled (no person can diminish you), Find things you do well and do them, take part in community and social activities, practice being a good friend and family member. <u>Do your deep breathing in clean air everyday</u> and at least three times a day! If you have forgotten how, start slowly and practice, practice, practice. Breath is life and life is precious. Allergies are not natural; they are signs of emotional problems...hey, if you want to argue...that is your other problem.

SECOND HAND SMOKE –
(NOT AN ALLERGY)

How often I have heard non-smokers trying to be polite and considerate of smokers declare that the "smoke doesn't bother them". How wrong they are! Some of them actually believe that second-hand smoke is not harmful. Where have they been for the past decade? SECOND-HAND SMOKE IS VERY HARMFUL AND CAN BE EXTREMELY DESTRUCTIVE. Any reaction to this is a sign your body is giving you to protect yourself from breathing this in.

First, it is unfiltered coming out of the "filter-less" end of the cigarette (and cigars and pipes are even worse). Not only the particles that cause asthma, emphysema, lung cancer and heart failure, but also the irritants that cause ulcers in the eyes, are being spewed out into the air you are surrounded with, along with over 100 poisons!

Stop kidding yourself...whether you realize it or not YOU ARE SMOKING RIGHT ALONG WITH THE SMOKER BY BREATHING IN THE SMOKE IN THE AIR. You are putting yourself at great risk of disease to your respiratory system along with your heart and eyes. There is no safe way to breath in tobacco smoke.

Next...even if you are stubborn enough to allow yourself to breathe in these toxic fumes...YOU MUST NEVER ALLOW CHILDREN TO BE SUBJECTED TO THIS ASSAULT ON THEIR TENDER BODIES! THIS IS CHILD ABUSE THAT CAN CAUSE IRREPARABLE

DAMAGE LEADING TO GHASTLY ILLNESS AND EARLY DEATH! NO EXAGGERATION IS BEING USED HERE. WAKE UP TO THE SCIENTIFIC FACTS. DENIAL IS INEXCUSABLE...TOO MUCH IS AT RISK.

I sincerely pray you now have the information you need to protect yourself and the children. Breathe the cleanest air you can find if you want strong healthy bodies for you and yours.

GRIEF

Effect on the Mind and the Body

It is firmly established that depression is the cause of many ills of the brain and the body due its weakening of the immune system. Grief is a severe form of depression.

If depression is not recognized and treated early, it can and does diminish the brain capacity causing poor memory, illogical thinking, irrational speech and behavior.

We see people who have suffered the loss of a loved one and with some; grief becomes a way of life. Whether it is internalized or very outwardly evident it is damaging the psyche (that which governs the total organism and its interactions with the environment). They must be helped by loving support from family and friends and wise professionals in the field of analysis. Those people, who can lead the suffering person to go forward in their life, realize they are loved and of worth, can help them to find new purpose and direction so they can heal the wounds of grief. Drugs should be the last resort.

The body reacts to grief very often by causing mucous to form in various parts of the body. With some it is in the bronchial tubes, others the lungs, or intestines and colon. These mucous formations can appear to be other ailments and very often are misdiagnosed. For example, mucous in the colon can be diagnosed as ulcerative colitis, which is an extreme disease requiring severe treatment including surgery, while mucous colitis can be cured in a two week period by simply taking a harmless substance called Saraca, which comfortably solidifies the waste material. How do I know this? This is my own personal history in that area. I diagnosed the ailment myself after reading in a magazine that happened to be available to me (I do not believe in coincidence) an article describing just my situation. I told the doctor what I felt it was since I had just two months before suffered the loss of my father at age 70 from kidney failure. The doctor was amazed at my pronouncement, but after all the tests were completed, he was delighted to tell me that I was right and he was wrong. Then in a very enlightened manner especially since this was in 1960, he exclaimed, "You willed it to be the lesser disease!" Amen.

So even with grief and depression we can use our will to overcome ills that seem to be drastic. Faith in God brings about seeming miracles but the miracles are the result of following Divine inspiration and wisdom and guidance. It is the natural path to healing the mind and the body. We must all work with the medical profession to broaden their scope of knowledge and wisdom. Keep an open mind so that the wisdom can come in.

FEAR

The kind of fear that rules peoples lives...like fear of illness, of loss, of failure, of success, of being alone, of being incapacitated, of being helpless (I can't begin to imagine all the fears that people carry in them)...if left unexamined and unexposed, not dealt with, can ruin their lives.

Living in fear, no matter what the reason, must be brought out into the open. Fear can become a habit. It can be taught. It also can be a magnet for exactly what we fear.

Faith replaces fear. Fear is a terrible burden that can either lead us to do unreasonable things or hinder us from doing things we need to do. When fear is replaced by faith we free ourselves to make wise decisions and take right actions.

When the fear is examined...held up in front of us to reason out...we can measure the extent of the effect of this fear. Are your fears keeping you from being all that you can be? Are you not going places you need to go for filling basic purposes? Are you taking unnecessary medication for fear of perhaps getting some illness? Are you submitting to drastic medical measures for fear of inheriting some illness? Are you neglecting your education because you think you can't "measure up"? Are you holding yourself back from advancement for fear of responsibility? Are you not using all of your talents for fear that you will be rejected? Are you holding onto relationships that are harmful to you for fear of being alone?

Fear can produce pictures in our mind that if concentrated on can be made manifest. Again...thoughts kept in mind reproduce in kind. Replace these pictures with things that can be accomplished with faith...things like perfect health, fitness and well being...Things like success, prosperity and popularity. Like confidence, poise and assurance...like feeling competent and skilled...like feeling loved, worthy and respected. The world wants you to be well and successful. Do your thing with faith in yourself and Divine guidance. That's right...you are never really alone. There is the greatest help in the world to get you over your fears. It is right inside you. It has worked for me for over 70 years. I know it works. Courage and faith produce miracles. You are entitled to yours.

ANGER

Another very debilitating emotion is anger. I found it very interesting to read that two renowned psychologists came to two diverse conclusions regarding the expression of anger. One, Paul Pearsall, Ph.D., felt that externally expressing anger is the harmful way of handling it, while the other, Dr. Abraham Maslow, expressed in his book, THE FARTHER REACHES OF HUMAN NATURE, that internalizing anger is the more harmful. Pearsall's book is the PLEASURE PRESCRIPTION. Except for the fact Maslow is deceased, I felt it would have been interesting to have the two of them discuss their research and how they came to their conclusions.

I mulled the two theories over in my mind and decided that it is the ANGER itself that is harmful no matter how it is experienced. The anger that is akin to rage can be devastating to the health of the individual whether expressed or not. Righteous indignation that is passing can be a venting experience and probably would not leave lasting damage to the person and can be an impetus to make necessary changes.

Holding anger for any length of time, especially accompanied by hurt feelings, feelings of resentment and revenge will ultimately cause mental, emotional and physical dysfunction. Clear thinking, appropriate speech, appropriate reaction or response will be difficult or impossible for the angry person to manage.

So whether the anger is left smoldering internally or shouted out at every opportunity, it is the emotion itself that must be looked at from every angle. First is it possible through meditation, deep breathing and positive affirmations that the angry person can find peace of mind so that new thoughts can be introduced? Second, if a lot of energy is being put into this anger, can this person be induced to exercise in some manner (walking, running, swimming, dancing, aerobics) to use up the bad energy in a good way? Can it be brought to the person's attention that his/her anger is endangering health and happiness to himself and that is too large a price to pay for this very unattractive emotion?

If you are the angry person, be your own wise guide in following these suggestions. Anger is not pleasant to feel or be around. Do not feel justified in being angry. Instead examine the alternatives of forgiveness, of being a peacemaker, of finding fair solutions to problems, of assuming loving attitudes and above all, feeling the joy of releasing the burden of anger. It is not a good weight to carry. As the popular saying goes "Get over it." Freedom from anger is a great blessing and opens the door to more satisfying emotions.

A LIFE WITH A LESSON

After having the rough manuscript edited, I was advised that I should reveal more of my own personal experiences while following the principles I have explained in the book. I had told the editor about several of the seemingly miraculous events that occurred in my life and he enthusiastically urged me to include them in this manual...so here goes.

I have already told you about my crossed eye straightening by my exercising it...but did I make it clear that it was by Divine Guidance that I knew to exercise it. The same manner of guidance helped me to straighten my very distorted back. Exercise and visualizing along with taking dance lessons corrected a severe case of what was then known as "sway back". I endured this unsightly posture from infancy to the age of 10 when I let Divine Guidance lead me to the solution. I was very aware of the guidance even though no one in my family spoke of such a marvelous power in the universe. So I know that from childhood when we are open to direct communication with God we receive our messages even if no one else in our family or among our relatives and friends is aware of such a gift. We all have it...it is just a matter of being aware of it.

When I was 31 years old I had moved to New York City to share an apartment with a cousin and her roomy. We three girls tried to be compatible in a small one-bedroom space (I slept on the sofa in the living room).

They worked days and I worked evenings so we seldom saw each other, but I would come "home" to a smoke-filled apartment and the stress weakened my immune system to where I managed to contract pneumonia. It was so severe that I was hospitalized for about a week. I came back to the apartment (a fifth floor walk up on 65th Street near York) all ready to start convalescing, but these were hardly ideal conditions to repair myself and I found myself with aching swollen joints from head to toe. I could not straighten my legs or use my thumbs. I convinced my cousin to get me an appointment at Bellevue Hospital with the head of the Physical Therapy Department (who was her boss). He diagnosed me with Rheumatoid Arthritis and told me it was not curable and that it would get progressively worse...but he arranged for me to go to New York Hospital three times a week for whirlpool and massage treatments to alleviate the pain and stiffness. So there I was in the middle of winter trudging the four or so blocks in the snow to the hospital three times a week. There were also the five flights of stairs to contend with and what is probably the most amazing feat of all...I was teaching dancing at the most exclusive studio in Manhattan on 57th Street off Fifth Avenue. Wow did I ever have to put on a cheerful look and force myself to go through the motions...but somehow I got through it...Until I decided enough is enough. I stopped the treatments at the hospital and made up my mind that God and I could lick this monstrous condition. I forced myself to have a better attitude about my living conditions (I asked my roomy to please air out the apartment before I came home and this helped tremendously. At least I could breathe!) The disease went into complete remission. No sign of it was left. The swollen knees and thumbs went back to normal and the pain was gone! Thank God!

A LIFE WITH A LESSON (CONTINUED)

I was so busy with my life, teaching dancing from about 1PM to 10PM at night and having a social life on the weekends that I refused to cater to any crippling disease. I pictured myself completely healed and let God do the rest. Now at 71, going on 72 years of age, I dance better than I did at 31. How's that for overcoming the "incurable". Is it any wonder that I cannot accept negative prognoses for me or for anyone else? The medical profession for the most part has not discovered the power of God to intervene in our behalf. I say for the most part because more and more the world of medicine is becoming aware of it...and for this I do thank God.

It would take another whole book to relate all my experiences but I will just include one more...a simple cataract operation that turned into the worst nightmare. Blindness! I had allowed myself to be convinced that I needed a tiny cataract removed. That was in my "good" eye, (The other one that had been crossed never regained full 20/20 vision because I heard the doctor tell my mother that it wouldn't and bought into that sad story). My "good" eye was the one that enabled me to drive a car and do the work involved with running my business, which for some 15 years was my only means of support. I ran a social club for non-smokers called The Healthy Set which involved contracts with hotels to hold the various dance parties and such and having to do all the publicity and accounting and correspondence...plus promoting my first small book which I distributed in the San Diego area where I lived and driving around to various lecture engagements.... In other words I NEEDED TO SEE! The ophthalmologist who operated on my eye was unknown to me but was recommended by my optometrist and I obeyed his instructions in good faith. Talk about misplaced faith in the medical profession...I take one of the prizes in gullible 101. What a sloppy job...Unbelievable! He didn't center the plastic lens properly. He pulled the iris and pupil up out of line with my other eye. He caused me double vision (I saw the full moon with a twin attached) and he did not suture the incision well so that it ruptured...My eye filled with blood leaving me completely sightless in that eye. I had to be rushed to the hospital to lie flat on my back for five days while the doctor kept telling me that he could not guarantee my sight and was so frantic that I had to calm him down and reassured him that God would not let me be blind. Each morning when I awoke a little more light was reaching the pitch black in my eye and finally after five days I could see again. Then my eyelid fell down over my eye and the doctor said that the clamp to hold it up damaged the muscle in the lid and there was nothing that could be done about it. Soooo...I exercised the lid and one day a sharp pain shot through the lid and it opened up! It is such a wonderful thing that God does not pay attention to the proclamations of the medical field and goes about healing the way it is intended. Again I say, is it any wonder that I place my faith in God rather than the Medical Profession. Be ye so advised.

A GLOBAL LOOK

Our view must never be limited geographically when considering the advancement of the human race. There are no boundary lines for air and water and the pollution thereof.

There are no boundaries for viruses, bacteria, and the like...

There are no boundaries for erroneous thinking (which is the worst pollution and greatest danger to the planet and life of its inhabitants).

If enlightenment comes to one country or to just a portion of a country, we can see that in order to have humanity as a whole ascend properly, it must not stop there. This is a planet-wide project.

Let us take a very broad look at the human race, please. With all the different races, languages, religions, cultures and political views, can we hope to unite humanity in the goal of higher consciousness?? The answer must be a resounding...YES!

We have been examining both the good and the harm we do to ourselves and to others. We have had our minds opened up to the realization that mistaken ideas cause mental and therefore physical damage to ourselves and damage to our environment.

The divisiveness that exists on the planet at present must not be a deterrent to the growth of the individual. Each one of us is responsible for his or her own evolution. In the pages of this book you have been told how you have powers that you may not have been aware of. You have been referred to books by famous people in the field of science that reinforce the knowledge that some of us have received metaphysically (beyond the physical). You have been made aware of how to use these powers to repress or activate genes, to rise above myths of heredity, to overcome illness, to slow down the aging process, to accept natural changes in the body as wise and good, to accept good health as a normal state, to accept Divine guidance in all matters and surely to be aware that there is a power and wisdom in the universe for good that you can and do have access to. We are coming to the closing passages of this book and I feel I would be remiss if I did not include all my thoughts on these matters. I sincerely want to be as helpful as I can be.

QUICKIES (FOR A SHORT ATTENTION SPAN)

**RIGID THINKING LEADS TO RIGID JOINTS (Be flexible in your thinking and keep a flexible body).

**IF SOMETHING IS ALWAYS EATING YOU, YOU COULD GET AN ULCER (Try to release the tension by not internalizing annoyances).

**KEEPING RESENTMENTS IN THE FRONT OF YOUR MIND CAN LEAD TO BAD HEADACHES (Let go of hurts and the pain will go as well)

**CARRYING AROUND ANGER CONSTANTLY AND/OR DEEPLY CAN LEAD TO CANCER (Isn't your health worth more than trying to justify your anger. Let it go.)

**FEELING PUT-UPON OR OVERLY BURDENED CAN LEAD TO OSTEOPOROSIS (Don't imagine yourself such a martyr AND realize that the responsibility is not all yours...or even part?)

**SELF-PITY OR FEELING THAT NO ONE CARES... OR LOVES YOU...CAN LEAD TO INTESTINAL PROBLEMS (If you are having digestive or elimination distress, know that you are loved and people do care)

**WORRY IS IMAGINATION RUN AMOK...IT ATTACKS OUR PEACE OF MIND (Protect your mind from worry by imagining all good outcomes)

**FEELINGS OF USELESSNESS AND HAVING NO HEALTHFUL INTERESTS CAN LEAD TO DIMINISHING MENTAL CAPACITY (Find interests that give you pleasure; do things that give you some satisfaction; be of help to others)

**NEGATIVE STATEMENTS BECOME REALITIES SO WATCH YOUR WORDS (We do live out our beliefs so believe in more positive results)

**IF YOU THINK THINGS CAN'T BE BETTER... THEY WON'T BE. (Try picturing a better scenario and act on it)

**IF YOU FEEL DISAPPOINTED AND EVEN DESPAIRING, YOU COULD WEAKEN YOUR IMMUNE SYSTEM TO BE OPEN TO ILLNESS (Take deep breaths, exercise, listen to beautiful music, dance, sing and/or do something that helps someone else feel good)

**HOLDING RESENTMENTS INTERNALLY CAN LEAD TO ARTHRITIS (Learn to forgive anything... and everything. Why keep rehashing old hurts)

**CLOGGED THINKING LEADS TO CLOGGED ARTERIES (Let new and better thoughts flow through freely)

**DIFFERENT FORMS OF RESENTMENT, ANGER, JEALOUSY OR DESPAIR, CAN CAUSE ALL SORTS OF ILLS INCLUDING DAMAGE TO ALL PARTS OF THE BODY AND MIND. DEPENDING ON THE SEVERITY OF THE HARMFUL FEELINGS, THE ILLNESS CAN BE PASSING OR CATASTROPHIC (Try to replace any and all bad thoughts and feelings with loving, caring, wise and understanding thoughts and feelings or you will possibly destroy yourself. We all have to pass on to the next dimension but we can do it in as good a shape as possible)

EASY OUTLINE FOR
HUMAN'S HANDBOOK

A. PHYSICAL
B. EMOTIONAL
C. MENTAL
D. SPIRITUAL

A. PHYSICAL

DO	DON'T
BREATH CLEAN AIR	BREATHE POLLUTED AIR
EXERCISE	BE SEDENTARY
EAT-NUTRITIOUS FOOD	EAT HARMFUL FOODS
GET SUFFICIENT SLEEP	DEPRIVE YOURSELF OF SLEEP
KEEP PROPER HYGIENE	NEGLECT CLEANLINESS
PROTECT EYES AND SKIN FROM SUN	EXPOSE EYES AND SKIN TO SUN
DRINK LOTS OF PURE WATER	BECOME DEHYDRATED
PURSUE HEALTHFUL ACTIVITIES	BECOME A COUCH POTATO
KEEP BRAIN ACTIVE	STOP LEARNING

PROTECT EARS FROM LOUD SOUNDS	EXPOSE EARS-TO EXCESSIVE SOUND
WEAR UV PROTECTED SUNGLASSES	ASSUME EYES ARE SAFE ON CLOUDY DAYS
WALK STRAIGHT POSTURED	SLOUCH AND SLUMP
TAKE GOOD CARE OF TEETH/GUMS	NEGLECT ORAL CLEANLINESS
WEAR A PLEASANT FACIAL EXPRESSION	LOOK GROUCHY
HAVE PURPOSE AND PLANS	FEEL USELESS AND LAZY
FIND-TALENTS AND INTERESTS	WASTE YOUR ABILITIES
BE GENEROUS, KIND AND HELPFUL	BE SELFISH AND UNCARING
WORK HONESTLY AND WELL	SLOUGH OFF DUTIES
BE DEPENDABLE	BE IRRESPONSIBLE
AVOID TOXINS IN ANY FORM	GET INTO DRUGS, NICOTINE, CAFFEINE; ALCOHOL ALL POLLUTANTS IN ANY FORM

B. EMOTIONAL

DO	**DON'T**
HAVE A FORGIVING NATURE	HOLD GRUDGES AND HURTS
FEEL LOVING AND KIND	HOLD RESENTMENTS AND VINDICTIVENESS
DEVELOP PEACE OF MIND	FEEL WORRY AND TORMENT
BE UNDERSTANDING	BE QUICK TO ANGER
BE FILLED WITH HOPE	BE DESPAIRING
FEEL YOUR WHOLENESS	FEEL FRAGMENTED
FEEL LOVED AND RESPECTED	FEEL SELF-PITY AND UNWORTHINESS
FEEL JOY	FEEL MISERABLE
FEEL COMPASSION	HOLD PREJUDICES
DEVELOP PATIENCE	BE TESTY AND SHARP TONGUED
BE COURAGEOUS	BE FEARFUL
REACH OUT TO OTHERS	BE INSENSITIVE TO OTHERS

C. MENTAL

DO	DON'T
KEEP AN OPEN MIND	KEEP A CLOSED MIND
LEARN ENLIGHTENED THOUGHTS	KEEP DARK THOUGHTS
USE GOOD JUDGMENT	MISJUDGE
LOOK FOR TRUTH	TRUST TO OLD MYTHS
STUDY, READ, LISTEN	NEGLECT LEARNING
KEEP AN ACTIVE MIND	KEEP AN IDLE MIND
USE THOUGHT CONSTRUCTIVELY	WASTE THOUGHTS ON USELESSNESS
RISE ABOVE NEGATIVITY	WALLOW IN MISERABLE THOUGHTS

KEEP HOPE AND TRUST	JUST GIVE UP
THINK OF HEALTH, WELL-BEING	THINK SICKNESS AND AFFLICTION
THINK YOUTH AND ENERGY	THINK AGING AND DETERIORATION
THINK KINDLY OF PEOPLE	GOSSIP AND DISPARAGE
FOLLOW YOUR BLISS	THINK THERE IS NO BLISS
PLAN A DAILY STRUCTURE	DRIFT WITHOUT MEANING
GET INVOLVED WITH USEFUL PROJECTS	GROW INWARD AND ISOLATED
KNOW THAT A MIND IS A VALUABLE THING TOO GOOD TO WASTE	LEAVE HOME WITHOUT IT

D. SPIRITUAL

DO	DON'T
KNOW THERE IS A POWER IN THE UNIVERSE GREATER THAN YOU ARE AND IT IS A POWER FOR GOOD	BELIEVE YOU ARE THE BE ALL AND END ALL
ACCEPT DIVINE GUIDANCE	IGNORE DIVINE GUIDANCE
MEDITATE AND RECEIVE WISDOM	CROWD YOUR MIND WITH HUMAN WEAK AND FAULTY BELIEFS
GO INTO THE SILENCE AND LISTEN	DEAFEN YOUR EARS AND SHUT OUT DIVINE WISDOM
EXPECT AND ACCEPT MIRACLES	REJECT MIRACLES
KNOW THAT YOU ARE A SPIRITUAL BEING IN PHYSICAL FORM	REJECT YOUR SPIRITUALITY

KNOW THAT
YOUR MIND IS
CONNECTED TO
THE MIND OF GOD

FEEL SEPARATED
FROM DIVINE MIND

OPEN YOUR MIND
TO THE WISDOM
THAT DIVINE MIND
IS SO READY TO
IMPART

BE SO STUBBORN
AND MISS OUT
ON THE BEAUTY,
INSPIRATION AND
LOVE THAT IS YOUR
BIRTHRIGHT

BE ALL THAT YOU
CAN BE

HINDER PROGRESS
AND THE
EVOLUTION OF THE
HUMAN/DIVINE
RACE

TO POST ON THE FRIDGE?

Dear Friend, are you..................................

> Walking and exercising in all kinds of healthful ways?

> Keeping your mind alert by using it constructively?

> Developing a positive attitude...about your usefulness...your abilities and talents?

> Eating a nourishing, healthful diet...in sensible portions?

> Considerate of your neighbors...and all others as well?

> Dependable and true to your words?

> Taking responsibility for your own well-being?

> Accepting your imperfections and those of others?

> Avoiding gossip and spreading rumors?

> Contributing your best to the community?

> Getting pleasure from accomplishing your tasks?

Learning from past mistakes so that you do not repeat them?

Telling your dear ones how much you love them... often?

Offering a helping hand when you are able?

Doing good deeds and enjoying it?

Examining what makes you angry and what you can do about it?

Making peace wherever you go?

Smiling more often than frowning?

Praising more often than criticizing?

Enjoying the beauty of your world?

Expressing gratitude to others for their kindness?

BIBLIOGRAPHY

(Hey...you don't have to take just my word on all this good stuff. Try reading some or all of the below listed books. Of course, we all have our own ways of expressing ourselves, but we seem to have a similar running theme... enlightenment).

QUANTUM HEALING and **AGELESS BODY, TIMELESS MIND**
Deepak Chopra, M.D.

SPONTANEOUS HEALING and **EIGHT WEEKS TO OPTIMUM HEALTH**
Andrew Weil, M.D.

TIMELESS HEALING
Herbert Benson, M.D

THE WISDOM OF THE BODY
Sherwin Nuland, M.D.

WOMEN'S BODIES, WOMEN'S WISDOM
Christiane Northrup, M.D.

MOLECULES OF EMOTION
Candace B. Pert, PhD

LOVE, MEDICINE AND MIRACLES
Bernie Siegel, M.D.

CHANGE YOUR BRAIN, CHANGE YOUR LIFE
Daniel G. Amen, M.D.

THE FARTHER REACHES OF HUMAN NATURE
Dr. Abraham Maslow

AS A MAN THINKETH
James Allen

JONATHAN LIVINGSTON SEAGULL and **ILLUSIONS**
Richard Bach

PSYCHOGENESIS
Jack Ensign Addington

THE EMERGING MIND
Karen Shanor, Ph.D

A SPIRITUAL SOLUTION TO EVERY PROBLEM
Wayne Dyer, PhD

Some of these books are new and some are quite old, but each came to me at a time when reinforcement of my beliefs was such a welcome gift. May the world continue to produce women and men who really seem to see the "light at the end of the tunnel" and express themselves so that the whole world might see as well?

HAPPY MIRACLES OF GOOD VISIONS COMING TRUE——A PARTIAL AUTOBIOGRAPHY

From my childhood up through high school, my life plan was to be an artist. I had shown this skill from the age of four. I loved drawing and later on, painting. I also had another picture of me being a musical comedy Broadway Star. That came from a talent for singing, dancing and acting. Being an extrovert, it turned out for the better that my parents decided I would not pursue the art career. Instead, they insisted I go to work in an insurance office, which of course I found extremely boring. So evenings I went to college to study art, and also for some years was actively involved with local theater groups in Albany, New York. Both of these activities gave me the outlets I needed to use these gifts. It helped me endure a most ungratifying office job for seven years.

Finally I had all I could stand of office work and turned to Divine Mind to lead me to work that would be more satisfying. I quit my job and went into a restaurant for dinner. There on the seat in the booth was a newspaper opened to classified employment ads. In large letters, I read "Arthur Murray Studio accepting applicants for teacher training." The studio was right down the street, so I went, got accepted right off and began what was to become one of the most enriching, satisfying and invigorating experiences to aid me all through my life. I needed the exercise after sitting for so many years behind a desk; I felt so good helping people learn to dance; and I became so proficient I was able to teach at the famous resorts in the Catskill Mountains. I had previously pictured myself doing that for years when as a vacationer at the resorts, I admired the beautifully costumed dancers on the stage. What a transformation from the girl in the business suit. The butterfly had emerged from the cocoon! (And I was soaring.)

Another happy vision was that of me in Greece. I felt I belonged there and received many signs leading me on. What a magnificent eleven months of living in that incredibly gorgeous country. Spirit led me, guided and inspired me to wonderful experiences. One of which was meeting the Greek "Adonis" I later married. He turned out to be just what I needed to help me along with my life at that time. We parted according to Divine plan, but those two years helped me to grow strong so that I became very capable of running my own business in San Diego for 15 years. It was a social club for Non-Smokers. It was so innovative, I was asked to be on TV and radio and also there were large articles in quite a few newspapers with my picture smiling out at the world. Hey, I was doing good work, and it felt wonderful. It led to my being a motivational speaker which was one of my greatest joys. When we go through the right doors, the way is made smooth to go farther. Spirit was leading me all along the way.

I was inspired in 1977 to write a small book entitled "Which End is Up?" which sold quite successfully in the San Diego area. I published and distributed it myself in

1981. By then I was 54 years young with another good ten years of success until I retired at age 64. Of course, I only retired from the club. I had lots of other projects envisioned for the future. Life is always renewing for me and giving me new starts. It does for everyone when you allow yourself to be governed by Divine Mind.

In 1991, I moved to Tucson to be near my family who had moved there shortly before. I had envisioned myself giving seminars to expand peoples' minds at the Udall Center. Even though I was told there would be too much red tape to go through to get in there, I went boldly to the Director and told her what I wanted to do. She loved it, and the vision became reality. As the lines to the song from <u>South Pacific</u> go, "You got to have a dream. If you don't have a dream, how you gonna have a dream come true." Sing along with me and let's make a joyous voice raised to heaven.

1995 came, and it was time for my 50th high school reunion in Albany. I became so nostalgic for my hometown, I moved back and stayed. Oh, what a good feeling to be where I have my roots. I don't like being so far away from my family, but Divine Mind is helping me. Soon after I moved to Albany, I became very involved with the ballroom dance groups here. I even started one of my own for about 1-½ years at a local nightclub, but that got sold and dancing just for pleasure is satisfying me now. I even got written up in a local newspaper as a phenomenon––a 73-year-old dance teacher and entrepreneur, and again I was pictured reaching out to the world, "Come join the joy." It really doesn't ever have to stop. Just envision and make it happen. Open up to receive it.

I must let you know about the miracle of having wonderful friends wherever I lived: New York City; Greece; Phoenix, Arizona; San Diego, California; Tucson, Arizona; and of course, Albany, New York. Divine Mind led us to each other. What a comfort, delight and support these dear people are to me.

The writing of this book for the past five years (so far) has been Divinely inspired and directed. And if all goes according to previous patterns, it will be actualized. God Bless.

EPILOGUE

WE ARE ALL STEWARDS OF THIS PLANET, BUT WE ARE ALSO STEWARDS OF OURSELVES. TAKE CARE.

IT IS TWELVE YEARS LATER—2010 THE SEQUEL TO THE HUMAN'S HANDBOOK THIS IS THE POINT

CHAPTER I

THE SKEPTICS:

Skeptical about what? How about the subjects in my original work of which this is the sequel? The responses I received ran the whole course from "It's all too good to be true. Miracles don't happen"... to "Are you trying to say I'm responsible for my problems?" Well, yes. So all those earthlings out there who still don't realize that their thoughts create the good and the bad in their life experience <u>are</u> "The Skeptics". Now, I could bang my head against a brick wall in frustration (actually trying to enter closed minds is the same thing), but, doubting is the fly in the human's ointment that keeps the "ointment" from doing its good work. So I wonder what the "Payoff" is for the skeptics who will not allow the "Good News" in; how about pains, suffering of many natures, senility, shutting down, or just producing very little, going through bad time after bad time. Oh, even my listing these things is not my nature, and if I didn't know how prevalent these symptoms are (even in minds that would seem much too young to accept them), I would just skip the whole situation. But I am a realist! (Don't laugh – meta-physics, which is my field, <u>is</u> the ultimate reality). If you live long enough and pay attention, you will be thrilled with this awakening. It is good stuff. There is no negativity. And if your mind is alert enough, there is no limit to what can be accomplished.

CHAPTER II

SOME OTHER BOOKS:

Titles, Authors, Quotes.

But do refer to the bibliography in the original manuscript. Treasures are listed in no particular order

BOOK: <u>The Third Chapter</u> by Sarah Lawrence-Lightfoot.:

My selected quote is: "We must develop a compelling vision of later life, one that does not assume a trajectory of decline after fifty but, recognizes this as a time of potential change, growth and new learning, a time when our courage gives us hope." Page 244. I would change one word and that would be <u>50</u> to <u>70</u>. My experience has shown me the world has accepted too young an age to think "old". My "70": is what some would consider "50". So here at 82 I am still writing and being published (albeit in a minor way) and dancing and helping the good ventures of others succeed. Oh, there is so much work to be done and I'm chomping at the bit ... to do ... to learn ... and so on..

BOOK: <u>The Art of Aging</u> by Sherwin Nuland, M.D.

My selected quote is: "But wisdom increases with age only for those who never lose their receptiveness to change, and to progress within themselves." page 272. I would add only that optimism is our best guide in this journey.

BOOK: <u>The Road Less Traveled and Beyond</u> by M. Scott Peck, M. D.

My selected quote is: "But we have the ability to alter human nature – if we choose to do so". page 211. I would add; the patience required comes from an outlook of optimism.

MY SUMMATION: To VISUALIZE the best result is to be on the path of ACTUALIZATION.

CHAPTER III

THE EVIDENCE:

Well here I am; Ms. Empirical Evidence Herself. And please don't be one of those "well that's just you" people. What I am the evidence of is not a singular event, nor a fluke of nature, nor some power bestowed only on me, nor the luck of the draw, nor my genes, (that's a goofy one). No my fellow humans it is Universal Law. What Divine mind has created it does not abandon. Take the blinders off and look around with your spiritual eyes.

Please let me refresh your memory regarding "My Miracles". The healing of that crossed eye, that crooked back, the rheumatoid arthritis, that blind eye, also the bonuses of the youthful appearance and energy, the rising up from the emotional ashes to really live enthusiastically, the dancing, the being able to be thrilled by great music, art, nature, laughter. Oh the gifts that prove we are blessed in so many ways

CHAPTER IV

THE FUTURE:

It is true I may not be able to change the mentality of an entire planet. That is not being pessimistic. Earth is what it is for some vast unearthly reason. But that does not mean a higher mentality cannot be achieved by a critical mass ... A mass of humanity that can make a difference in how the human race is evolving ... So that there is hope for better health, better morality, better ethics, sane minds. In future generations wisdom will no longer pass through the earth invisible so that no one can see it, but rather seep into the mind of the receptive so that ignorance will be washed away in a tide of enlightenment. Humans will at last enjoy more fit bodies, better attitudes, clarity of purpose, strength of convictions, joy in achieving goals, compassion free of all prejudice, sanity that cannot be shaken by the madness it encounters, peace.

CHAPTER V

THE CHOICES:

A choice: Close your mind to new thinking (which in reality is very ancient thinking). If you refer to Plato you will find thinking that now, centuries later, is still being ignored; a wisdom that does seem to have gone through the earth invisible. You have the choice not to read, not to learn, not to grow... stagnation!

BUT

You also have the choice to hunger for learning, growth and enlightenment.

You have the choice to open up to a realization that there is a power and presence in the universe that is our help and guidance at all times. You have to be quiet. Quiet your human thoughts and allow a greater Divine mind to enter your thoughts. Breathe deeply and repetitively; let go all tension, anger, frustration, hopelessness, and do surrender to magnificent ideas. Take on the power to do good for all.

CHAPTER VI

WHAT IS YOUR PROBLEM?

Only you know what is going on in your mind. Whatever façade you are displaying, whether cheerful or sad, may not be the root emotion you are really feeling.

It is the root emotion that affects our physical condition, our life experiences and our final result. So many things affect us in our life outwardly, but the root cause is the one that requires complete honesty. It is between you and your mind. Let down the barriers of denial. Have a good cry. Surrender to peace, and be willing to try "a miracle".

CHAPTER VII

TRANSFORMATION:

<u>All it takes is to experience a miracle, and recognize it</u>. A miracle by some definition is the unexpected outcome of a certain situation – for the better. Because it is so unexpected, "Miracle" seems like the only explanation to the unenlightened. However, when one experiences multiple "miracles" such as unexpected healing, help in the time of need, the right person at the right time and place, the right job or idea to start a business, the impetus to move on, the strength to accomplish tasks, one knows.

Are you getting some idea of "Miraculous" events. Well, be you transformed by the renewal of your <u>MIND</u> because <u>that</u> is where it all begins. When you open <u>your</u> mind to <u>Divine Guidance</u> it is revealed to you and you know what to allow happen and what you are to do. This is truth. Tear down the obstacles and move on.

CHAPTER VIII

THIS IS WHAT I KNOW:

From what I hear how some (too many) people express themselves. The mind of earthlings seems to be trapped in a kind of limited thinking. They cannot accept a new idea. And that would not be so tragic except for the reality of the human condition. The smug attitude that screams out "I am helpless in the face of conditions. See how smart I am that I know that". (Unquote)!

There really are more things in heaven and earth than are dreamt of in their philosophy; a whole world of personal power ... A world where Plato's "Aha" sensation is the most blissful and enlightening and empowering. So what if for over a couple millennium this has been ignored. So what if the human brain is shackled to the limited and harmful ideas of primitive theories. What is real is ignored and in its place a limited, false, restricting way of thinking is implanted in their brain. Of course they have the confused and twisted minds of some erroneously labled pundits, authorities (otherwise known as scientists, physicists, M.D.s and the like) who are like robots teaching and imposing their harmful ignorant false "facts" to back up what they think is knowledge. That is the human race's most crippling fact of life ... The so called knowledge and quasi facts of the smug but terribly wrong "authorities".

I would rather look to Abraham Mazlow, or Deepak Chopka, or Candace Pert or Sherwin Nuland OR Why don't the closed minded folk try understanding what these people are trying to tell them. Please before it is too late open your mind to real universal truth. Live on this planet in an expansive, productive, exciting manner. Help create a civilization that is truly civilized. It has been said "earthlings have gone from barbarism to decadence without even touching on civilization". Well, look at it: The sophisticated masses high on alcohol and drugs, the violence committed by the people in power, the over indulgence in themselves and the neglect of the rest of society. How about all the hundreds of thousands maimed not just in pointless wars, but in the hospitals by the so called careless caregivers.

This truly does appear to be the planet of the insane. G.B. Shaw said it his way years ago and not knowing he had, I also proclaimed it and now Eckhart Tolle has expressed observations likewise.

What a great idea if saneness could overtake the planet like a wonderful and welcome divine healing. I'm for that – but first we have to admit the "sickness" to allow the healing to begin

Here is a test to see if you recognize the symptoms: (check true or false for each)

T	F	
_____	_____	I am not responsible for any adverse condition in my body
_____	_____	I do not have any power to correct any adverse condition in my body

_____ _____ My mind does not affect any condition in my body.

_____ _____ My mind does not affect any situation in my life.

_____ _____ I should always accept a medical professional's opinion

_____ _____ The world's situations are no reflection of human attitude.

_____ _____ I do not have to learn any "new" ideas that would upset my mindset.

If you marked "true" to any or all of the above, you are really confused!

Truth is the opposite of these statements!

A LOVE LETTER TO HUMANITY

Dear Ones,

How I long to hear your voice, see your face; know you have awakened. I long to share the wonders of the world with you. Together we can lift up the mantle of darkness and let in the light of Divine wisdom. It is always there. How good it is that we in our quiet times can receive our messages from such a wonderful, powerful and loving SOURCE. All the answers to the universal dilemmas are around us for us to just <u>LISTEN</u>. I love to be comforted and inspired and energized by the wisdom our SOURCE pours into our mind. We share a love that is so great that surely it can overcome all separation, all doubt, all obstacles, and create a new and finer world for humanity to truly enjoy. I believe God gave us love to solve the human problem. Let us use it together

I love you,

Marian